The Mind's Eye
Theatre and Media Design from the Inside Out

Wayne Kramer

D1314518

HEINEMANN
Portsmouth, NH

Heinemann
A division of Reed Elsevier Inc.
361 Hanover Street
Portsmouth, NH 03801–3912
www.heinemanndrama.com

Offices and agents throughout the world

The author and publisher wish to thank those who have generously given permission to reprint borrowed material:

Excerpt from *The Berlin Stories* by Christopher Isherwood. Copyright © 1935 by Christopher Isherwood. Reprinted by permission of New Directions Publishing Corp.

Excerpt from *The Glass Menagerie* by Tennessee Williams. Copyright © 1945 by The University of the South and Edwin D. Williams. Reprinted by permission of New Directions Publishing Corp.

Excerpt from "Most Wanted Paintings" by Vitaly Komar and Alex Melamid. Copyright © 2002 by Vitaly Komar and Alex Melamid. Published by the Dia Center for the Arts. Used by permission. *http://www.diacenter.org/km/surveyresults.html*

Excerpt from *Waiting for Godot* by Samuel Beckett. Copyright © 1954 by Grove/ Atlantic, Inc. Published by Grove/Atlantic, Inc. Reprinted by permission.

Library of Congress Cataloging-in-Publication Data
Kramer, Wayne.
    The mind's eye : theatre and media design from the inside out / Wayne Kramer.
        p. cm.
    ISBN 0-325-00640-7 (alk. paper)
    1. Theatres—Stage-setting and scenery.   2. Theatre—Production and direction.   I. Title.
PN2091.S8K6926   2004
792.02'5—dc22   2004004801

Editor: Lisa A. Barnett
Production editor: Sonja S. Chapman
Cover design: Jenny Jensen Greenleaf
Compositor: Valerie Levy/Drawing Board Studios
Manufacturing: Steve Bernier

Printed in the United States of America on acid-free paper
08   07   06   05   04   VP   1   2   3   4   5

Contents

Preface: Eyeing the Camera

I am a camera with its shutter open, quite passive, recording, not thinking. Recording the man shaving at the window opposite and the woman in the kimono washing her hair. Some day, all of this will have to be developed, carefully printed, fixed.[1]

from "A Berlin Diary (Autumn 1930)"
The Berlin Stories by Christopher Isherwood

The playwright John van Druten turned Christopher Isherwood's Berlin Stories *into a successful play titled* I Am a Camera. *The play became a movie and, subsequently, a Broadway musical titled* Cabaret, *which, again, became a movie.*

Some years ago, I was working at Universal Studios on a now mercifully forgotten comedy, doomed to failure, but with a cast, director, designers, and crew of remarkable skill and talent. I remember walking with the production designer scouting locations, trying to find existing facades and terrain appropriate for the film. Every once in a while he would hold his hand up to his right eye and cover it. I worried that something was wrong and asked if I might help. He said it was no problem. "I am being the camera." I must have looked puzzled because he then explained. When he was looking for particular exterior locations he did not want to be distracted by his binocular vision process. Our two eyes allow us to see in three dimensions, giving us the sense of depth. The camera sees with one eye, in monoscopic vision. You can try this yourself. Scan the room or space you are in now with both eyes. Try to register the sense of the space. Now close one eye and do the same thing. The images are quite different.

At another time I was watching this same production designer do a made-for-television movie. The soundstage sets were a courtroom and a jail cell. The designer seemed to be paying particular

---

[1] Christopher Isherwood, "Goodbye to Berlin," *The Berlin Stories* (New York: New Directions Publishing, 1963), 1.

attention to the colors of the wainscoting as the stairs descended into the jail cell. I asked him about this and he explained the progression of the palette (the arrangement of colors) he had established for the narrative movement from the courtroom to the jail cell. This seemed so like the conversations I would have in production meetings for theatre productions. I somehow had thought film and television would be different.

Some years earlier I had talked with a former Broadway designer who had given up that career and moved to California to do game show designs for television. What must that move have been like? What principles of design addressed the demands of a game show differently from those expected of a Broadway play? How did the video camera shift the use of design elements?

These experiences prompted my thinking about the design process. When are the decisions connected to a design process the same? When are they different? As designers we all employ the same basic elements and tools of the design process. The medium in which they are used (theatre or film or video or video games or website design) will impose certain restrictions unique to the technology of that medium. But the early responses are too similar to ignore as a pattern and as a strategy. If, as designers, we can get a grasp of the design elements, then we can adjust them through the filters of the different media. The raw material of our work, how something will look, will be half done. The medium in which we are working will complete the process.

This book, then, is about how to understand and explore a method of design. It is about rethinking how we approach design because we must reinvent the theatre and its images.

It is perhaps ironic that theatre becomes the touchstone for discussions that include design in new media. The theatre, as a social and communal art, is constantly shifting in response to societal concerns and the aesthetics of presentation. Theatre artists are constantly looking for new and more successful ways of communicating ideas to an audience. It is an old truth in the theatre that today's innovation in presentation or writing will, with repetition, become tomorrow's cliché. The search for new ways of presenting ideas and information in the theatre relies on the theatre artists' ability to redefine the performance space, the script, and the nature of the interaction with the audience.

Just as we now live in a more geographically mobile world (we move around a lot), so too we've discovered discipline mobility (we change jobs a lot). It is a simple fact that people often end up doing jobs they did not anticipate doing. Some of this migration and mobility is based on opportunity—we work where we are given the chance. Some is based on the similarity of techniques among disciplines that allows us, as designers, to move fluidly between jobs.

To this reality we can bring a particular set of design skills, basic in organization and scope, that can inform our work in various media. We no longer separate the set designer for the theatre from the art director for film. The art director for video games uses the same basic designer tools as the television art director or the costume designer. Each medium imposes its own technical limitations or advantages, but the good designer can, and does, move more freely among them. The nature of distribution for film, video, video games, and the Internet has created many more opportunities for design than the theatre alone could hire. This media explosion has contributed to the migration and mobility. There continues to be a need for designers in all these areas, and the alert student of design will grasp the basic principles of the design process and filter them through the technical expectations of the medium.

The discussions in this book are complemented with a CD-ROM that should help illustrate those design elements that often seem to elude accurate verbal discussion. In an effort to locate where the process of design is similar but where the product is wholly different, this book concludes with case studies offered as models for beginning designers in the paths and choices particular designers have experienced.

—Wayne Kramer
Amherst, Massachusetts

Acknowledgments

This book would not have been possible without the help and encouragement of many people. I am indebted, especially, to Elly Donkin and Nina Payne for their help with the manuscript; to the Marion and Jasper Whiting Foundation, whose support helped launch this investigation; and to Hampshire College for their faculty development grants.

I would like to thank all those professionals who took time from their busy schedules to talk with me and share their perspectives for the next generation of designers. Especially I would like to thank Stephen Marsh and Ted Cooper, whose early encouragement and conversation sparked my interests. I would also like to thank Mark Thomas of Microsoft for his help; Kym Moore for her special help; Louai Abu Osba for translating my CD storyboards with style and wit; and Lisa Barnett for her careful readings and advocacy.

And finally I would like to thank all my students who, over the years, have been my best teachers.

Introduction: The Mind's Eye

Hamlet: My father—methinks I see my father!
Horatio: Where, my lord?
Hamlet: In my mind's eye, Horatio

from Hamlet
by William Shakespeare, Act One, Scene Two

Design is fundamentally a way of looking at something and sharing that perspective with others. It is a creative response to an idea. Unlike the visual arts and crafts where this process is wholly proprietary, design for the theatre, film, and electronic and digital media is collaborative. The author's intent, the client's directive, and the other collaborators mediate both the process and the result.

Design is the act of illustrating the intention of the author, and through that act of illustration, communicating an understanding of what the author intended. By intention, we mean the reason the work was created. This constitutes one of the important distinctions between what can be described as art and craft. It is generally assumed that the intention of art is to comment on some aspect of the human condition. These aspects of the human condition might include, for example, observations or meditations on love, hate, war, death, envy, fear, courage, or corruption. We may identify with and see ourselves in the death of the leading character and realize, for example, the consequences of betrayal. We may become relieved over the realization that others share our sense of inadequacy. We may remember with affection our first love and its difference from that portrayed in the narrative.

In the decorative arts and crafts, the intention is usually grounded in the pure aesthetics of design. Aesthetics might include sensuous line, evocative textures, explosive colors, or pleasing shapes. We can respond to the purely tactile sensation of the woven basket, the play of color in the hand-dyed silk scarf, the sensuous flow of the grain in a wooden desk. The object creates a pleasurable sensation. The senses are stimulated in some combination of the visual, the aural, the tactile, even the olfactory.

There is a certain act of clairvoyance the designer engages at the beginning of a project, the ability to see into another space and time, to visualize future events through the lens of the text with the intent of the author. This is an act of ideation. The specificity of this vision, the degree of detail, the resonance with the project's intent—these identify the successful designer. For the distinguished American playwright Edward Albee, the best design "is that which illuminates without intruding and vanishes as the play emerges."[1]

When we talk about intent, we are assigning a purpose to the work of the writer, the conceptualist, or the client. What is the reason for this work? Why was it written? What is it trying to say to us? Sometimes this will be clearly evident, as in "Please buy our soap" or "Think again about the consequences of not being loyal to your friends" or "Winning this race will really make me feel better!"

Obviously these generalizations will meet with contradictions and exceptions. We are trying to draw fine lines between areas of gray in the hope of creating black and white. But the process of this attempted separation can clarify our thinking and inform our strategies for design. In some of the media, we are asked to look at information, ideas, or entertainment but without the direct assumption of changing how we think about the world or our place in it. We are not casting aspersions here nor trying to establish a hierarchy of value. Such judgments are better left to cultural critics and those who vote awards. There can be plays that do not change how we think but merely make us laugh. There are news broadcasts that can change the way we see the world. Certain video games, like morality plays, can teach us about loyalty, betrayal, or self-reliance. But as a generalization, we can say that the performing arts, including film, television (situation comedies, espisodics, and soap operas), and theatre, are asking us to think about our lives or the lives of others differently.

Other theatricalized events and electronic or digital media can also have intent. Our obligation as designers serving these areas is to determine intent, whatever the venue, and use that as a starting point, a launching pad, for the design process. The case studies at the end of this book will help illustrate this process, whether staging a parade, doing a museum exhibit, designing a video game, or introducing a new product through a staged event such as an indus-

---

[1] Edward Albee, "Re: Interview," Correspondence with the author, 30, July, 2001.

trial. The template for each of these processes is the time-honored design strategy of theatre design.

If the designer can isolate the intention, then the job of designing can begin as a synaptic response. It is possible to make connotative associations with the message and the medium we will be using. We might call this process the mind's eye. Hamlet (in the quote cited at the beginning of this chapter) is saying he saw something in his mind. The external sensory process was appropriated as an internal response. The act of "seeing" was reallocated to his "mind." The events, for Hamlet, had conspired to create not a real event but an imagined event. In the same way, when we enter the script or narrative—that is, when we begin to discover the interiority of the play—we begin to make connections between our own experiences, the narrative, and the presumed intent of the author. Some of these connections will be denotative. They will be explicit. One problem for beginning designers is that they are presented with an overwhelming sense of choice. They become paralyzed, not from a lack of ideas but from an overabundance of possibilities. Something needs to intercede, to bring a kind of hierarchical order to the choices. Locating connotative values will begin the editing process. Connotative values are implicit—that is, not stated, but implied by the combination of different pieces of information.

This is the same process as that of the director and of the actor, but with different tools. The director will work with the raw material of the production (design, acting, staging, conceptual rhythm, and style) and the actor will work with the raw material of acting (voice and body through emotional and intellectual connection and recall). The author may be a playwright, a screenwriter, a website client, a corporation, or video game producer. Using the tools of the discipline, the designer is trying to communicate an understanding of the intention of the author, one that will help others understand that intention or take some action because of it. Most designers, directors, and actors also believe, and rightly, that their work will more effectively communicate that intention than the written word alone. If the narrative or description of the work implies that it is to be seen, it will need to be realized by the designers. If the intention of the author is communicated through a variety of means, from several directions and sources (both visual and aural), the possibility for retaining the intention longer is greater.

For our purposes, the intention of the author is the first step in responding. The next stage is the beginning of the design process, the design response. This sequence of responses can be arranged as follows:

We begin with a script (or an idea).
↓
There is a first analysis.
↓
To this we offer a first response.
↓
This will lead to a first conference, a sharing of that response with others.
↓
This will lead to a second response, one that incorporates ideas from the first conference.
↓
This second response is often altered or enhanced by an understanding of the limitations (financial, logistical, conceptual).
↓
There is a third response.
↓
There is an execution of the response.
↓
This execution may lead to a fourth response, in process.
↓
Upon completion of the project there is usually a final response, an evaluation.
↓
The evaluation can shift how we respond the next time (this could mean an Emmy, an Oscar, a Tony, or no job next week).

Begin with a Script (or an Idea)

This comes in various forms. It can be a script, original or published. It can be several thousand years old or brand new. It can be a treatment study for a television series. It can be a commercial script with a storyboard and dialogue. It can be a two-page proposal for a treatment of a video game. The form of the "script" will vary widely.

But in each of these instances the beginning of the process is some statement of intent or action, implied or overt. As designers, we will begin to create images and form associations between images based on the information given us.

First Analysis

Our analysis of a script can be divided into two stages: There is a precognitive stage where we respond instinctually and intuitively to the tone, mood, and feeling of the script. We may describe this feeling as invoking generalized emotional or aesthetic responses. The play seems dark and bitter. The script seems upbeat and happy. The play seems introspective and psychoanalytical. The play is straightforward and invokes feelings of childhood. The writing seems very political and polemical. The script is complicated, with twists and turns of events. The rhythm seems like a maelstrom, an inevitable momentum to conclusion. These generalized reactions and feelings then move to a cognitive stage, where we begin to figure out the meaning. This is a critical stage because it is here we begin to identify the intent of the script or the author. Why was this written? What are we trying to achieve in this project? What is the purpose of the event? What are we trying to say? These may or may not seem obvious but our job as designers is to name the intent. By looking at the various levels of intent we will begin to establish the interiority of the event, script, or idea. This means we will begin to explore all the ramifications of the intent. What are the various reasons for the project and how will our design help that process?

Much of design work should be about finding "entry points" into the script. Metaphorical response is one. "This play is like a baseball game, with opposing teams and clear objectives." Or "This play is like a car wreck: unanticipated, unexpected action and dire consequences." We might ask, "How do the characters talk? How does the narrative move (rhythm)? Where is the setting? How is it described? What is the sense of progression of events? What happens first? What happens next? What happens finally? When was the work written? How would this work change my life? How do I want an auditor or an audience to react to this? What is the driving force in this work? What is its *raison d'être* or justification?" These questions begin to shift our relationship to the writing, to the script.

We move from a passive, detached tourism to an active partnership with the playwright.

First Response

Having explored the questions above, we are ready to catalog, in a conceptual way, the answers. Often, this will be through establishing that metaphorical response. What do the themes of this performance work remind us of? We can begin to organize our thoughts and random images. The more we design, the more quickly these images will come to us and the more quickly we can catalog them into recognizable and manageable units of visual information. A method of design allows us to assign metaphorical responses to this script and then to begin breaking down that metaphor into manageable design elements.

As we begin confronting the intention of the project, we will automatically begin to generate images. These are an internalized inventory of our collective responses to the world around us. They can be mundane, complicated, simple, or profound. We carry with us, at all times, images and associations that have been forming all our lives: the particular color of a rose, the feel of granite, the sharp edge of a knife, the softness of a well-worn blanket. Sometimes these images are associative. We remember them in terms of an event: the use of upright gladiolas at a funeral, the sharp pain to the knee when we fell on the sidewalk, the shock of a knife cut to the hand, the warmth of sunshine through trees after a first-date picnic.

Sometimes we remember them simply because they appealed to our senses: the rough texture of tree bark, the color of the mountains at sunset, the edginess of a picket fence, the sensuous warmth of hand-rubbed wood.

This first cataloging of images should be as uncensored as possible. We may be seeing the event on a wide field of wheat. If the event is to be staged in an eight-by-ten room, this may be impossible. But retain the early images as long as possible. You may be able to retain the sense of the response and replicate it, not literally but figuratively.

Let us imagine ourselves as designers working on a new script. The script suggests a cityscape. The narrative of the script suggests connotative values that render this cityscape as fearful, decaying, and endangering. How can we communicate this range of emotional responses in a way that will catalog them conveniently in a single creative "folder"?

We can borrow from the process of the poet and apply a metaphorical reading to the idea (the text). The text is like . . . (then we fill in the blank). By looking at what happens to the characters, by looking at the narrative, by looking at the implications of the characters actions, we can form a conclusion that will encapsulate these responses into a metaphor.

Let's say we are working on the musical *West Side Story*. We might conclude the metaphor is "shards of glass." The setting is urban. The musical is about the tensions and dangers of living in the city and finding happiness in a world torn by strife and hatred. Relationships in the narrative seem to be triangulated. Two people are trying to get together but a third person is always intervening.

Glass is an important image of the cityscape. Broken glass is even clearer as an image. Shards of glass, the triangulated pieces that result from the broken glass, suggest more imagery. They are elongated triangles. They are sharp. The lines can suggest a strong movement, a direction, an arrow pointing. The shards are threatening. The surface of the glass may be reflective. It is hard and yet transparent. The glass may remind us of the reflected gasoline rainbows that so often appear in the collected puddles at a curb after a rain in the city. The phrase "gasoline rainbows" has a tension. We do not associate gasoline with rainbows. The phrase evokes the mundane and the beautiful, the prosaic and the ideal. The glass can break up the spectrum into a range of colors but the glass is still broken. And so the designer may come to the production meeting with a suggestion that the images for this script may be like shards of glass.

This process can do two things. It can facilitate communication within the design group and within the production team. Designers can talk to each other using the metaphors as a kind of short hand. Designers can talk with producers or directors using the spoken language as shorthand for the visual language. "Is it heliotrope or aubergine?" can be a confusing discussion outside the designer circle. But if we talk about the metaphorical response to the play, if we can find the handle for our discussion that all can grasp, we may become clearer and more focused in our thinking.

The metaphor in the earlier example, shards of glass, will help cohere the responses of the various designers. Our inventory of design element choices (transparency, spectral colors, sharp edges, triangulated shapes, reflective and hard surfaces) will control the individual responses of the designers in a way that registers similarly with one another. And so, like the individual painter who can control all elements of a piece into a single cohesive statement, we can as a collection of designers control the look and feeling of our joint efforts with a similar coherence. If this is in the service of the writer's intent, we may increase the ability of the audience or the individual to understand the writer's purpose, the writer's intent.

First Conference: Sharing the Response with Others

As designers, the private act of responding to the script or event will eventually need to go public. We will need to share what we are thinking, our perspective. The more flexible we are at this stage, the more successfully we will integrate our work into that of the other designers and those who are on the collaborative team. We may have several ideas. As we generate ideas we may stimulate the thinking of the other members of the team. New ideas and possibilities will emerge. These collaborative exchanges may involve several meetings or may break down into more individual meetings.

Collaboration is like a search for the Holy Grail. It is something that we often try but rarely achieve. When it does happen, it is exhilarating. Good collaborative experiences teach us about our craft. We meet other designers and conceptualists whose ideas and insights challenge and stimulate us. If we are lucky we form bonds of friendship and colleagueship that serve us well in future enterprises. Collaboration feeds us artistically. Our next project is a search for the same magic, the same successful combination of listening, contributing, and creating.

Second Response: Incorporating Ideas from the First Conference

These discussions with the other members of the project will inform us differently than when we were thinking by ourselves. New insights may be offered. A new way of seeing the project may emerge. Our original ideas may become the core of the project, may be altered by the visions of the group, or may be thrown out. But unless we offer ideas and enter the process we will not be contributing to the project. This is not a time to be quiet. By offering ideas and images we are clarifying our own thinking; by articulating our responses we are stimulating the thinking of others. In this way, we are bringing responsibility to our membership in the collaborative.

Understanding the Limitations (Financial, Logistical, Conceptual)

At this point we have been thinking and imaging broadly, without limitation. But soon we will have to think more concretely, as we move to the prospect of realization. "What will the project cost, as we have been discussing it? Can we afford it? Is there another way to do it? What is the time frame for the project? Do we have enough time to plan and execute the project? Are our designs realizable? Is the size of the performance space too small for our ideas?"

Third Response

Once the collaborative enters into the discussion of limitations, we begin to revise our responses. Our design work is edited, trimmed, refined. We will often find that our original ideas and those of our colleagues are now shifting to a more collective response. It often becomes hard to separate our design ideas from those of the people we are working with. We have melded into a creative whole, a new aggregate of focus and direction. The sense of territoriality will lessen as we subscribe to a larger, revised, and more collective vision of the work ahead.

This collective movement to a kind of artistic consensus can be called the "conceptual stage." The group begins to subscribe to an overarching vision, like an umbrella, for the project that may be metaphorical, stylistic, attitudinal, emotive, psychological, or any combination of those. We have already looked at metaphorical response as a designer's individual reaction. Now we are looking at collective reactions, a series of convenient shorthand phrases that begin to identify the emerging group's approach, the concept. Examples of this shorthand might include, "Maybe we should think of this project as a deep forest with softly filtered light but the characters can't get out." Or maybe the group finds phrases like "It's very urban and gritty and assaultive, maybe we should go with that" or "We need to think of the play as satire, either light and social or scathing and political." "The script is dark and foreboding; we know what is going to happen. It's inevitable." "This play is really a statement against apartheid." "The script is more a comment on relationships." "The play is really circular, characters turning in on themselves or the ending bringing us around full circle." "The play is really in the lead character's head. It's all an aberration." These become the handles that allow the group to effectively and efficiently manage the range of decisions that now must be made.

Execution of the Response

This is a time to produce, more concretely, the designs we have been discussing and formulating. Whatever the personal form of our design work, we will need now to offer our own design response in a form the others can see and understand clearly. This is a transition from the verbal process to the visual process. We are switching languages. The previous dialogue we had will now comingle with the visual dialogues we will have with our colleagues. We may offer sketches, models, storyboards, swatches of fabric, media colors, elementary mock-ups, and illustrations from other sources.

We are beginning to concretize the discussions we had earlier into specific design choices. Sometimes this stage of our work is the most frustrating. Words have their own connotative and imagining power. Some of our colleagues are more comfortable with words and have filled in their own specific images. At this point, what we offer may be confirming of earlier discussions, move those discussions forward into visual choices, or cause concern because the images do not mesh with previous conceptions. But this period of transition is an important one, as we move from word to image, and we need to keep returning to our earlier discussions as a touchstone, a reference point. We need to return to that space and spot where we all began.

Fourth Response: In Process

No design remains the same. There will always be circumstances and events that cause us to revise our work in process. New ideas emerge and, yes, mistakes are made. New constraints impose themselves. Our thinking changes.

Final Response: Evaluation

Usually we think our work is done when the project is completed. But in fact, our work continues for some time, often years. We need to evaluate what we did, how it worked. Or how did it not work? How could the process have been changed? What would we do differently the next time? Did we learn something new as designers: new strategies, new materials, and new methods? Did we learn something about how to find the interiority of the script or the project? Did we evaluate the intent correctly? Did we learn something about how we communicate with our colleagues? Did we find new ways of communicating our visions and our designs?

Next Time

Each of these questions will begin the process of revising our next design project or how we approach that project. We may have learned new tricks or methods. We can add these to our inventory of tools and strategies. We may have learned what to avoid or how to rethink our responses and design choices.

Once we begin to understand the sequence of our responses, we can begin to adjust our position in each for a more successful and rewarding design response. By looking at the sequence of our activities in designing, we can begin to isolate particular moments and then determine where our energies are best expended to facilitate our work as designers. Some of us will want to spend more time practicing our articulation skills, our ability to explain what we are planning or thinking. Some of us will, as designers, need to spend more energy on rendering skills, life-drawing skills, or model making. Some of us will have to work at maintaining contact with colleagues in the first stages of our work. The analysis of our effectiveness at each stage will assure that our next project, as designers, will be even better.

If we can, as designers, develop a strategy for response, a way of looking at the project and translating that into our own visual perspective, and if we can analyze the tools of design in a personally useful way or if we can segment our work as designers into stages of collaboration and response, then we are at the crossroads of choice. We will have developed a set of tools and techniques that may hold us in effective stead with the developing technologies and markets.

Design choices apply whether you are designing a stage set, costumes, lights, navigation buttons for a website, the look of the film, the game show podiums for television, or the rock wall textures for a computer game. Design choices are dependent on design elements as a lens for communicating intent. The designer becomes a guide and should lead us to a better understanding of the event or the activity.

Design for media rarely stands on its own. It is in service to actors, directors, other designers, navigational strategies, corporate intent, playwright intent, programmer intent, and screenwriter intent, and it is constrained or liberated by the scope of the technology.

The response sequence just offered has a range of variables and implications. We can begin with the first, the script. This first step does presume the designer can determine the intent. Through discussions with the client or the production team, the purpose, at some level, needs to be determined.

The lesson here is important. The design technology will change; there will always be new challenges and new ways of presenting information and ideas. But the design principles will remain the same. Master the design principles and you can navigate the new technologies with confidence. With that in mind this text will use the design process for theatre as an example of how design strategies can apply to various media.

The second half of this book examines specific designers working in a variety of media. In terms of these case studies, the most recent technologies seem to be invoking the oldest design traditions. People who are working on game design at Microsoft are also talking enthusiastically about going to the art museums and being recharged by looking at artists' work from the past. Art history is informing website design. They are also talking about the need for collaboration.

What Is Design?

This book is written for people who want to be designers. The organization of the ideas reflects a belief that there are basic, fundamental similarities between the design process in the theatre and the design process in film and in electronic and digital media. These similarities are grounded in the coherent use of design elements, the fundamental building blocks of the designer's process. Further, the basic assumption is that the purpose of design is to illuminate, to illustrate, the intent of the author, whoever or whatever that might be.

Design in these terms is visual. It is about the process of exploring design elements in combinations that create connotative value and meet the primary objective: explicating the intent of the author. Others may benefit from an understanding of this process. Directors can benefit from learning the language of designers. They can also learn about connotative value in visual composition. Other designers (such as interior designers, architects, public space planners, and so on) can also learn from the process of design for a performing medium. Playwrights and writers may learn about more effective ways to use space and location.

This book then is about a set of tools derived from one of the oldest art forms (the theatre) in the belief that they can serve the newest art forms. We will investigate a set of strategies for finding meaning in the script. We will search for guidelines that encourage a collaborative process that will cohere the project. And, finally, we will look at a group of designers and practitioners who use those strategies in their professional work.

1
Design Elements

Bottom: I will discharge it in either your straw-colour beard,
your orange-tawny beard, your purple-in-grain beard,
or your French-crown-colour beard, your perfect yellow.

from A Midsummer Night's Dream
by William Shakespeare, Act One, Scene Two

What are the design elements? At its most fundamental, a design response to a text or an idea is a reshuffling of the components of design into a new order, a new set of relationships. Each design project calls for a reshuffling of these elements because each new project calls for a new approach, a new way of thinking about the text or ideas, a new objective. For the purposes of our discussion, design can be broken down into a series of categories that interact with each other, support each other, and redefine each other.

This is one list of design elements. Various media will establish other lists and include other categories. The categories listed here are areas of design that seem to translate most effectively between media and therefore warrant study and familiarity. These elements are:

Color
Line
Shape
Texture
Balance and proportion
Movement
Contrast and variety

By breaking down design responses into a series of categories and choices, we can begin to understand some of the intuitive process that all designers go through in giving form and interpretation to text and ideas.

As with any process of construction or creativity, knowing the basic tools of that process and how to use them are the keys. Understanding the nature of these tools, their properties and functions, as well as our responses to them, will give substance and support to the process of interpretation. Good design begins with a full understanding of the elements of design and continues with being conversant in the properties of each. Designers will make choices in emphasizing one design element over another or establish a particular feeling or attitude to the work by formulating a particular combination of elements.

This chapter discusses the elements of design as general categories. It will be useful to supplement this reading with the CD-ROM provided with this book as a way of visualizing particular aspects of the elements. Discussions of movement, for example, are best supported with actual examples of something moving. These discussions of design elements are introductory. Not all categories or possibilities are discussed. These are broadly defined categories, and each designer in response to the text or project explores the details of each. All designers gain experience and insights into the design elements by working with them. Their use will become intuitive and less self-conscious as the practice with them, the experience in application, becomes more extensive and repetitive.

It is in the particular combination of design elements that designers demonstrate their skill in rendering the meaning of the text or project, the intent of the writer, or the vision of the director. Combinations of design elements create emotional values, cognitive (thematic) values, aesthetic values, and psychological values. If we begin by saying that a particular design element, such as color, can elicit an emotional response or a particular feeling, then we can begin to catalog the range of those colors and emotional responses. If we continue by ascribing cognitive value to the same sets of design elements, we begin to align those design elements as prompts for a particular kind of perception or invoking a particular memory.

Psychological values in design elements fall somewhere between the emotional and the cognitive. Psychological responses to design elements invoke instinctual responses and behavioral associations. Aesthetic values in design elements are perhaps the easiest to identify. We know what colors we like. We know what shapes give us pleasure or seem intimidating. A particular combination of colors can make us feel fearful or happy. A particular combination of lines can suggest regimentation or tell us where to look. Certain textures can make us feel apprehensive or we may simply delight in the recollection of the pleasures of feeling one of those textures. Good design will take these responses into account and orchestrate them into a meaningful and useful set of design choices.

Design elements can be thought of as the modifiers and adjectives in grammatical sentence construction. Let's start with a simple sentence:

The girl sat under the tree.

We have a subject (*the girl*). We have an action (*sat*) and we have an object (*the tree*). No doubt as you were reading the sentence you formed an image, either specific or general, of the situation described. We can think of this simple sentence as the text. But we are still missing information. What is the intent of the author? What is the implied meaning? How should we react to this information? What should we learn from it? The degree of increasing specificity we establish will make the meaning clearer. Notice the shifts that seem to occur in the sentence when we add something.

The little girl sat under the tree.
The teenage girl sat under the tree.

Already the meaning is shifting based on the new information; the adjectives we are adding seem to change the circumstance and the character of the event and the way we respond. The *little girl* is perhaps alone and we should worry. The *teenage girl* is perhaps reflecting and we are intruding. We might continue.

The little girl sat happily on the new grass under the blossoming apple tree.
The teenage girl sat sadly on the snowbank under the drooping pine tree.

Now each sentence has new information and takes on a wholly different meaning. We still have the same information we had in the first sentence but it has become modified by additions and changes in tone or feeling. Each new variation or addition has changed the mood and the feeling of the sentence, even the meaning. We begin with the sentence (the text or the idea). We determine the intent of the author. We explicate that intent with modifiers. This is the process of design and the modifiers and adjectives are the design elements.

This system of modifiers can be made more specific, now, to the design process. Suppose the script describes the following: "Character One enters the door." We have, again, been given some information. But is there more? What kind of door? Where does the door go? What's on the other side of the door? Is the door merely functional or is it also decorative? What is Character One wearing? Is the character coming inside from the outside cold and snow? Is the character entering a conference room full of expectant clients? Is the character trying to escape? Does the door seem to bar the escape? All these modifiers change the simple script description in the same way the simple sentence we earlier offered was changed by details and modifications.

Think of the play or the project as you would the development of the sentence we just looked at. The script is the sentence. It offers us important and basic information about the narrative, the plot, or the idea. When we add producers and directors we begin to offer an attitude to that sentence (that action or event). We begin to figure out the intent of the author. What did she mean by the sentence? What is implied? What is unstated? How do we think this sentence will affect our viewers or our audience? What do we want them to think about this sentence? As designers we add our own responses to these questions and then we begin to articulate that response with specific design element choices. These choices begin to change or to augment the information the sentence offers. By looking at the design elements as having characteristics and values, we can develop an inventory of design tools that are a response to the particular event or production.

Emotional Value

Certain design elements can elicit emotional responses. The color red, for example, can suggest feelings of fear (the sense of danger), apprehension (again, the sense of danger), or joy. The texture of concrete slabs can suggest something painful or impenetrable. Curves and circles can suggest comfort and security. These emotional values are partially cultural; a specific group gives values to the elements of design. Some are associative; the design elements remind us of other things in our lives, our environments, and our experiences. Red, for example, can be associated with the color of blood, which, in turn, can suggest anger (a flushed state), pain (a wound or cut), or pleasure (a kiss).

Cognitive Value

Certain combinations of design elements can lead us to think in specific ways about the text or the project. Cognitive value usually relates to the intent of the project or the design, the implied meaning. This sense of the thematic content of the work is "telegraphed" or transmitted by the combinations of design elements to the audience or the viewer. For example, strong, repetitive formal lines can suggest containment, formality, regimentation, or authority. A sense of balance can suggest formality, dependability, security, or stasis. A sense of imbalance can suggest corruption, dynamism, catastrophe, or impending doom. Certain colors can suggest renewal and growth while others may invoke ideas of decay and death.

Psychological Value

Somewhere between the emotional responses to the text and the thinking responses to the design (the thematic implications) resides the psychological response. This value shares traits of both. The design elements, their combinations, create in us a sense of relatedness to the text or the idea. We begin to understand the intent or the effort in terms of our own experiences and feelings. This is behavioral (our sense of our own behavior and that of others); the attitudes and actions can be associated with a mental state of awareness or existence. Certain design elements may invoke our responses to authority or danger. They may intensify our feelings about murder or love. Certain combinations of emotional and cognitive responses will coalesce our feelings of retribution or reconciliation.

Aesthetic Value

Sometimes it is just the sensual pleasure of the design elements that gives weight and importance to the text or the project. We may simply enjoy or delight in the interplay of color shifts, the variety of textures, or the playfulness of lines. These are values that do not relate to other conditions or memories. They reside alone as sensory pleasures, in and of themselves. A combination of design elements can often suggest where to look. A key value of visual design is the ability to direct the gaze and the attention of the viewer. Determining what is most important to look at and then finding ways to get the viewer to do that are key components of any design project. Certain repetitions of color, for example, can keep the viewer focused on particular areas. Certain combinations of line can move the viewer's eye along logical and predictable paths.

Connotative Value

We can combine all the aforementioned values into the general category: connotative value. A basic tenet in the discussion of design elements is the principle of connotative value. Design elements, at one level, can have explicit, denotative values. The color red is different from the color blue. The line can be described as a curve or a combination of lines as a triangle. Design elements can also have implicit or connotative values. This value layers on the design elements those qualities and associations that produce feelings and memories. Sometimes these values are cultural. In Western culture, the color white is often used at weddings as a signifier of purity and innocence. Such a color in Chinese culture would signify death or something funereal. The manipulation of connotative value in design elements is one of the most powerful tools a designer can employ.

Note also that connotative value is strongly influenced by the context in which it is perceived. That is, the script will influence how we think about or react to the design elements. Often design elements will have conflicting or concurrent connotative values: dynamic or threatening, comforting or smothering, active or unstable, supporting or impeding. It is the context in which the elements appear, the script, that begins suggesting or connoting a particular feeling. For example, in one script the strong use of diagonals in the set or on a particular costume or in the direction of the light may suggest dynamism, enthusiasm, and rigor while with another script, with different reinforcing ideas and language, the same diagonals will become threatening, unstable, and insecure. The script, the thematics, and the intent of both the author and the production team mediate this bipolarity in connotative value.

Color

This is the most basic and most easily recognized of the design elements. We all have responses to color and can easily identify it as a design element. In a survey conducted by Vitaly Komar and Alex Melamid for the Dia Center for the Arts in New York,[1] results suggested that out of fourteen countries surveyed, blue was the most popular color. Green ran a close second in most countries, and red became a more distant third. It is interesting to speculate about the significance of such an overwhelming preference for blue. Clearly, color is at the forefront of most people's conscious thinking about design and design elements. We walk into a room and notice the color, usually, as a first response to a design choice. While the lines of the room, the balance of the proportions and the texture of the walls will come subsequently, if at all, the identification of color is usually immediate and conscious. Because of this, manipulation of color is central to the design process and a key factor in creating a response to the text or project.

Properties of Color

There are several ways to explore the elements of color. Most systems or theories of color establish two broad categories initially. There is color in pigment and there is color in light. The basics are different in each. Design areas such as costumes, sets, and props use pigment color. Fabric is dyed with natural or aniline dyes to change or give it color. Sets are painted with pigmented binders to give them color. Lighting instruments interpose a color medium between the light source, the lenses, and the object focused on. Some of the principles for these two forms of color are different. Many are the same.

Color can be further divided into categories of primary and secondary (even tertiary) and complementary based on their combination. Primary colors are indivisible. They are not combinations of other colors. Notice that primary colors are different for pigment and for light. In pigment, the primary colors are red, yellow, and blue. These are the basic building blocks of color in pigment. These pigment primary colors cannot be reduced and are not the result of

---

[1]Vitaly Komar and Alex Melamid, "Most Wanted Paintings," *Dia Center for the Arts* (2002), *http://www.diacenter.org/km/surveyresults.html* (24, June, 2002).

combining other colors. That is why they are called primary. Combinations of these primaries will create other colors. If we combine red and yellow, we get orange. Orange is identified as a secondary color. If we combine red and blue, we get purple, which is also identified as a secondary color. If we combine yellow and blue, we get green, another secondary color. If we combine all the primary and secondary colors we get black.

In light, the primaries are different. They are: red, blue, and green. These are not combinations of other colors. Note especially that green is not a combination of other colors, as in pigment. Again, these are the basic building blocks of color in light. Combinations of these primaries will create other colors. If we combine red and green, we get amber, which is identified as a secondary color. If we combine red and blue we get magenta, also a secondary color. If we combine green and blue we get cyan, another secondary color. If we combine all the primary and secondary colors we get white light.

Often these differentiations of primary and secondary colors are arranged in a sequence as a wheel. The color wheel allows for quick identification of primary and secondary colors and complementary and contiguous colors. Complementary colors appear opposite each other on this color wheel. Contiguous colors appear next to each other. In pigment, the complementary colors are orange and blue, yellow and purple; red and green. In light the complementaries are amber and blue, magenta and green, red and cyan. In pigment, yellow and orange or yellow and green are contiguous colors as are blue and green or blue and purple. Red and orange or red and purple are also contiguous. In light, contiguous colors are amber and red or amber and green, cyan and green or cyan and blue, and red and magenta or red and amber.

We have just divided pigment and light into various colors, or hues. Hue is one way of describing color. It is the name given to a specific color, for example: "red." These colors can be further divided into other categories: value and intensity.

Value is often described as the degree of saturation in a color, that is, how the color moves from light to dark, its grayness. The value of a color can be determined by how it is located between white and black. If a color moves more to white, we call it a "tint." If it moves more to black, we call it a "shade."

Intensity in color (also called "chroma") is the descriptor we apply to the apparent brightness or dullness of the color. This is sometimes described as the purity of the color. Colors can be dulled by the addition of another color.

Beginning designers will more readily recognize hue as the basic description of color. Increased use and experimentation will help distinguish these other characteristics. Recognition of the other characteristics of color will increase the options for the designer, especially in a design element so easily recognized by the viewer or the audience.

Colors acquire connotative value. Often this is associative. Have you ever wondered how the choice of colors for the traffic intersection lights came about? Why do we stop on red and go on green? Why don't we stop on purple and go on blue? Originally, the concept of colored lights to dictate traveling behavior resided with the railroad companies. Red was fairly easy as a color choice to designate "be careful or stop" for its associative values with danger or blood. But the next choice, the color for "all okay and move forward" was white. This color became confusing with cars and houses in the area of the signals (with predictable and sometimes disastrous results) and so green (originally used to suggest caution) was selected to mean go. When streets became congested with cars and needed signal controls, these colors were borrowed from the railroad system. Today, we automatically associate red with stop and green with go. We have been habituated, through use and association, to think of these two colors in particular ways.

Colors associated with water, for example, are considered "cool" colors. Blue would be considered a cool color. Colors associated with fire are considered "warm" colors. Red is considered a warm color. Green is considered a cool color. Gray and silver are often associated with man-made or technical objects such as steel and chrome. Green and brown are often associated with elements in nature, such as grass and trees. Colors such as purple or crimson are often associated with historical usage, such as royalty or privilege. Because the original organic source of some of these colors (such as shellfish) was restricted, the association was made between access and the "right" to use the color because of one's status or position.

Some colors have emotional connotations. Red can be thought of as hot-blooded, passionate, energetic, or fearsome. Green can be considered moderate, calm, new, and fresh or, in some connotations, envious (primarily from linguistic use as in "green with envy"). Blue can be associated with calm, peaceful, pleasant, or cold. Yellow is usually thought of as happy, positive, or sickly and dangerous. Colors that seem to move between two polar opposites are often chameleon-like, that is, they seem to take on the characteristics of colors around them. Yellow, for example, can seem warm and happy, especially if it is seen in proximity to red. With green, the yellow will become cooler. Purple will seem warmer when seen with red and cooler when seen with blue. Any discussion of color characteristics needs to identify the "neutrals": black and white. Usually these are classified as the presence of all colors or the absence of all colors. Black and white can assume neutral characteristics in any design plan—that is, they can be used with other colors that have connotative and associate values without distracting from those values.

It is important here to acknowledge that good design will often contradict these assumptions about connotative and associative value. Just as we may become comfortable with always thinking of white as a color for innocence and purity, some enterprising designer will use it for an opposite, subverting purpose. Design is always changing and evolving with the cultural assumptions and associations as well as with boredom and predictability. An understanding of some of the connotative and associative relationships of color is not the concluding solution. It is just a beginning.

With such a wide range of colors, it is often difficult for the designer to make choices. Again, the designer should return to the script, the text, and determine those characteristics and attributes of color that seem to resonate with the intent of the author. Such a determination will inevitably lead to a specific set of choices for color. This elimination process can be described as creating a palette. The term comes from the flat, wooden traylike device painters would use when working away from their studios. By introducing just those specific colors they wanted to work with, the painters would spread an amount of those pigments on the palette. Combinations of these limited pigments produced the painting. Using the same process, designers can restrict their use of color in a particular design by selecting a limited number of colors. Often these choices will involve primary and secondary colors that have been affected by value and intensity. Such slight variations will keep the sense of variety in the colors but will also relate them to each other and create a sense of uniformity and coherence in the design.

Color-coding is another way to employ color as a design element in the service of the text or project. *Macbeth* is a play about the increasing temptations and seductions of power. Lady Macbeth is often portrayed as sinking, along with her husband, into a trap of deceit and murder. Designers will often introduce this idea into the costuming by having Lady Macbeth appear, at first, with small accents of red in her costuming. As the play progresses, she appears with increasing amounts of red, all the way to her famous line, "Out, damned spot! out, I say! . . . Yet who would have thought the old man to have had so much blood in him? . . . Here's the smell of the blood still: all the perfumes of Arabia will not sweeten this little hand." Lighting designers can collude in this process by changing the palette and intensity of the lights.

Equally, another of Shakespeare's plays can offer examples of the usefulness of color-coding. *Romeo and Juliet* is a play about two warring families. The audience needs to be able to distinguish between the members of each family. Costume designers will often design one palette or set of colors for the Capulets and another palette or set of colors for the Montagues. This helps provide a visual reference point for the audience, especially in the earlier and larger encounter scenes with several members of each family.

Color can also be used to mark the progressions of plot or character. The lighting can move from color to color as a way of marking physical, emotional, and psychological change. The costume colors can mark the same transitions. A character may start out in lighter colors and, as the play progresses, appear in darker colors. The set may do the same, with palettes progressing from setting to setting.

This sense of color progression can be a means to coherence and a way to suggest transitions. We might call this a "progressive triad." The designer begins with three colors as a beginning control over palette (note that these can be either three distinct hues, or three variations on intensity and value, or two colors with variations for the third). To this first palette, the designer offers a second palette (to be used in either another set or another costume or a shift in the light plot). For this second palette, the designer can take two of those colors and add a new, third color. Then taking the newest addition and one of the older colors, a third palette can be created with the addition of yet another color. This progression of additions and deletions from the triad palette can create a sense of coherence and unity to the progression of the design. The viewer will take the original colors as a reference point and move through the progressive triads smoothly and without interruption. The opposite can also be used. The palette for one section can be contrasted (with completely new colors) with another section as a statement of difference and change.

Line

Line can be either actual or implied. An actual line inscribes the distance between two points. That inscribing can be on the horizontal or the vertical, along a curve, or on the diagonal. Just as the name implies, a horizontal line follows the horizon, that is, from left to right or right to left. In following the line we move our heads back and forth. A vertical line moves up and down. In following that line we move our heads up and down. Diagonal lines connect differing positions between the horizontal and the vertical. Line can also be a curve or a combination of curves. Line allows the eye to follow a directed path, like a car to the highway. Movement along that line can be playful, rigid, curvaceous, angular, or repetitive.

The inscribing of the line between two points can also be implied—that is, the line is not actual but is inferred from the relationship between other objects. For example, we may see a line of trees along the street. The implied line of the group of trees is a horizontal line. Like connecting dots, we connect each tree to the next one with an implied line. Conversely, each individual tree can have an implied vertical line. We connect the total volume of the tree, starting at the base, continuing through the trunk and into the topmost branches as a vertical line, reaching up. The individual tree has one kind of implied line and the group of trees has another kind of implied line.

Properties of Line

In design work, lines are often combined to form new combinations. Curved lines can be joined into a snakelike pattern or into a circle or ellipse. Horizontal and vertical lines can be combined into a grid pattern or random matrix. Horizontal and vertical lines can also be combined to form a stair step, a ziggurat pattern, or a crenellated edge.

These various combinations of lines begin to elicit associations that have connotative value. The horizontal line suggests the ground, the solid earth, and so offers the sense of stability and solidness. The vertical line suggests moving into the air, moving up, and so offers an inspirational or aspirational connotation. Curved lines suggest comfort and security, as being enfolded in someone's arms. Groups of lines, combinations of different actual and implied lines, can begin to suggest other values. A whole group of vertical lines can seem prisonlike, invoking the images of cell bars, or military-like, invoking the image of a row of flags or spikes. Often vertical and horizontal lines can seem static or stable. Diagonal lines seem active or unstable. They seem to be moving between two points, not yet horizontal or vertical, or they seem to be falling, losing their position.

Certain types of lines or combinations of lines can invoke associations with the natural world or the man-made world. Curves, soft angles, and apparently random combinations of lines can suggest the biological or botanical; they remind us of body shapes and plant formations. Sharp, machined angles and straight lines suggest a manufactured or technical association. These are, of course, generalizations. A craggy rock outcropping can have sharp angles and almost straight lines and a series of jacquard-woven drapes can have soft flowing curved lines. But the larger generalizations can offer clues to general associations that might be useful in making certain design choices.

Line can enter the design process in several ways. It can be implied by the aggregate of shapes and forms in the design. The setting, for example, could be primarily vertical or primarily curves. Line can also be literal in such things as the details of surface ornament and piping on a dress, the surface detail in the scenery, or the dominant direction of the lighting. In this way line can also help establish focus onstage; that is, the combination of lines or implied lines will help show the audience where to look. This is a strategy taken from painterly techniques where the key element of the painting is the point of focus because the painter has used line, real or implied, to direct our gaze.

Just as line was implied by the row of trees on the street, so too line can be implied in a set by the combinations of other elements. Two major distinctions in theatre work concern the relationship of the set to the proscenium arch, the framing of the stage picture. Historically, realistic sets used the illusion of parallel lines to establish a box set. The upstage wall seemed to parallel the line of the proscenium arch, and while the other walls were splayed or angled out to present a better view for more audience members, the general feeling was one of straight lines either parallel or perpendicular to the proscenium arch. These large flat walls were broken up visually with jogs, architectural protrusions, and alcoves or small changes in the surface to relieve the monotony of large flat surfaces. A significant shift in this arrangement with the proscenium arch has been the use of the diagonal. Borrowing from the visual language of the director and actor where diagonal crosses and moves can seem more dynamic and active, the realistic set can be rotated so the major angle of the set is on a diagonal to the proscenium arch. The implied diagonal line of the set offers a newer dynamic and a more active visual picture.

Shape

Shape results from a combination of lines that when connected form an outline. In two-dimensional form we see the object with width and height. These shapes can be circles, squares, rectangles, octagons, and triangles. Vertical lines combine with horizontal lines to become squares and rectangles and triangles. Curves combine to form circles. In three-dimensional form, when objects acquire not just width and height but also depth, these shapes become cubes, pylons, spheres, and pyramids. At times we recognize individual shapes. However, we can also ascribe shape to a collection of objects, just as we did earlier with line. The objects may be gathered together into a wholly different shape. Image a room full of beach balls arranged in a conical shape. Or imagine a series of pylons (rectangles) arranged in a semicircle (curves).

Shape can also be used to describe the body silhouettes (like drawing an outline of someone's full body shape) and facial constructions or physiognomy. Such terms as *chunky, hourglass, rail-like,* and *pear-shaped* have been applied to our physical shapes. The generalized "t" shape (with the shoulders creating the horizontal and the torso the vertical) can be expanded to include body outlines that seem to match in some ways the geometrics used in set design. Bodies can be squared, circular, rectangular, and triangular. Costuming can create silhouettes that alter the body shape. These same geometric shapes can be layered on faces. High foreheads and broad brows can create a triangular look, especially with weaker chins. Broad brows and strong chins can create a more rectangular look. Faces can also seem rounded or elongated.

The rendering of shapes in two-dimensional media (such as painting and computer screens) has created a whole lexicon of dimensionality. Using the principle that parallel lines seem to converge at the horizon line, shapes can be drawn to simulate this effect (linear perspective) and therefore suggest depth and dimensionality.

This effect is easily recalled by thinking of a street in a large city where the street itself seems to converge at the horizon and the buildings recede in apparent height as they too near the horizon. Long stretches of road in a flat landscape (wheat fields) will allow for the same effect, with the road seeming to get smaller and end at the horizon line. The addition of chiaroscuro to these shapes (rendering with color and value to create light, shade, and shadow) will increase the sense of dimensionality.

Shapes also have mass and both the individual shape and any collection of shapes will acquire a sense of visual weight and volume. This sense of mass will contribute to another design element: balance and proportion.

Properties of Shape

As with line, shapes acquire connotative value that is associative. A large rectangular box, following the horizon line, will assume the characteristics of stability and solidness. It does not appear to be falling over. An upright pylon, following the vertical line, will appear aspiring and reaching. A pylon tilted on edge will appear about to fall or actively thrusting up. This can lead to connotations of instability, weakness, and chaos or active, dynamic, and energized movement.

Combinations of shapes can have equal connotative value. A group of circles or spheres can suggest happiness or playfulness (in their association with balloons or groups of flowers) while a group of cubes can suggest formality and rigidity. Groups of shapes that are arranged following particular line patterns (horizontal, vertical, diagonal) can also acquire new connotative value as a group, connected by the implication of those lines. They can appear regimented and constricting or less regimented and casual. They can seem chaotic or spontaneous and free-spirited. Groups of shapes can also suggest harmony or tension. Classical Greek architecture employed the visual relationship between the strong vertical lines of the columns with the stabilizing rectangles of the base stairs and the softening conclusion of the triangular pediment at top that does not seem to truncate the columns but allows the eye to move upward and conclude gently. This sense of harmony and stability invokes associations with security and authority. These same invocations are still seen in the classical facades of banks and courthouses.

Certain combinations of shapes can, as with line, suggest elements from the natural world or the man-made world. Strong rectangular, cubic, and squared shapes (geometrics) seem more machined or man-made. More free-form shapes, with their random outlining, seem organic, as with leaf shapes and boulders. Again, the connotations for each will differ. Organic shapes can seem wild, uninhibited, and freeing or dangerous, unpredictable, and threatening. More formal shapes can seem stabilizing, authoritarian, and secure or overbearing, rigid, and implacable.

Texture

Texture refers to the surface of an object or the aggregate effect of a group of objects. For instance, we can describe the surface of a piece of velvet as soft and sensuous. We can describe a scattering of fallen autumn leaves as crunchy and edgy or serrated. In the first example, the velvet surface evokes memories of what that surface felt like. That in turn becomes associative. The velvet is pleasurable and offers rewarding sensations as we rub our hands across it. The fallen leaves each have an individual character and outline but the combination of whole groups of leaves renders a new surface, an aggregate surface that takes on a new character apart from the individual character of each separate leaf.

In design, texture is most often recollection. Most of design is still connected to the visual and the aural. The tactile is inferred. We remember what a surface felt like. We remember the tactile sensation. By extension, it is connotative as we remember the unpleasantness or pleasantness of the surface. These characteristics can be used to affect. The large mass of a textured surface or a contrast of textured surfaces can be intimidating, frightening, substantial, all-powerful, caressing, comforting, sensuous, and pleasant. Texture also adds depth and detail by offering surfaces that take light differently, in different planes, and therefore creates contrast and interest.

We can ascribe certain qualitative values to these textures around us based on our sense of tactile recall and associations with similar surfaces from the past. We remember how something felt in the past and associate it, often, with an experience. Our early memories are of things soft and comforting. As infants we were coddled in our mother's arms, wrapped in soft blankets and treated to gentle touches. We began to associate these textural surfaces with comfort, pleasantness, and desirability. So surfaces like new leaves, velvet, silk, cotton batting, and feathers invoke positive feelings. If, as a child, we have fallen while skateboarding on the sidewalks, we may remember concrete as hard, unyielding, and abrasive. Conversely if we watched our house being built from the concrete basement up, it can be remembered as durable, substantial, and reliable.

Texture can have an organic character with invocations of bark and leaves. It can have an industrial character with machined surfaces and metallic reflections. It can suggest wealth and power as with polished marble surfaces or a lowly state with battered and weathered wood siding. In clothing, texture can suggest refinement and sensuousness as with satins and silks. It can suggest power as with leathers and metallics. It can suggest authority as with brocades and velvets; or the simple and unpretentious as with ginghams and the weaves associated with homespun or monk's cloth. Textural surfaces that are hard and unyielding, soft and draping, scratchy and rough, or smooth and polished can each invoke specific feelings and associations.

Texture is an important design element in video design, especially in video games and digital film work. Textures can offer a sense of verisimilitude to objects that are seen in two-dimensional form. Texture mapping to polygons has become an important part of rendering the environments of video games as well as scenery and persons in digital film work. The textures lend depth to the two-dimensional rendering of these forms and truthfulness or acceptability from the observer's point of view. Of equal importance is how the textures can be read. We see textures as shifts in light, shade, and shadow. The hills, valleys, ridges, and creases and polish or fuzziness of the surfaces we describe as texture are perceived through the play of light off these surfaces. Lighting and, especially, the direction of lighting play an important role in convincing us of the textural qualities. In theatre, these textural surfaces can be rendered with paint or actual additions of dimensional media to replicate or suggest textures. By offering a measure of detail and layering, texture can begin to add depth and visual interest to surfaces and objects.

Properties of Texture

Textures can invoke memories and associations. Texture can define the surface of individual objects or become different as the surface of a group of objects. Textures that are soft and yielding can suggest vulnerability and sensuousness. Textures can be organic, of the natural world, or geometric and of the man-made world. They can relate to intent, aggression and submission. They can invoke psychological feelings of apprehension and fear or indulgence and comfort. Texture can create interest by offering the eye a variety of surfaces and, therefore, becomes less predictable.

Balance and Proportion

Balance can be applied to a variety of design elements or combinations of elements. In this sense it is an organizer. Balance ascribes weight to various objects and then creates an imaginary fulcrum point to balance those objects. At its simplest, balance is a seesaw. An object (or person) on one side of the balancing point, the fulcrum, needs an equally weighted object (or person) on the opposite side of the balancing point. This will equalize their positions. If one of the objects is substantially heavier than the other, the balance is off and the seesaw action stops. In design, the seesaw, the line of balance, is implied but can still be sensed. It is not seen. The objects have a relationship to each other that we infer by their apparent visual weight and then their sense of balance or imbalance.

The apparent visual weight of an object is determined by its visual dominance—that is, how it demonstrates properties of other design elements to attract our attention. There can be a sense of balance between colors, between lines, between shapes, and between textures. Objects that seem to be of approximately the same size and weight are visually equal. They do not have to be the same. For example, a circle and a square of the same relative size will have the same approximate visual weight, just as two circles or two squares of the same size will have the same visual weight.

When standing, our bodies are engaged in a continuing act of establishing balance so we do not fall over. Balance is an intuitive part of our perceptions. Objects and spaces that appear balanced create a sense of harmony, stability, and assurance. If the objects appear imbalanced, the connotative values are of instability, apprehension, or movement away from stasis.

Balance can also be imposed on groups of objects or masses of other design elements. A group of pylons on one side of the stage or screen can be balanced by a similar or different group of objects, but with the same visual weight, on the other side of the stage or screen.

Balance can also be imposed by the principle of negative space, or spaces without objects. This is sometimes a harder principle to grasp. When we see an object in a given space, the total volume of that space is redefined. The part of the space that is unoccupied takes on weight by the sheer volume it presents in comparison to the object. So an object alone stage left or on the right side of the screen will seem to be in a balanced picture if the volume on the stage right or left side of the screen is proportionate. The volume of the negative space needs to be larger to seem balanced with an object. Just as with an old-fashioned set of scales, we can add weight to each tray on each side of the scale and create a balanced or imbalanced state. Sometimes it is simply a matter of changing the size or numbers of objects to achieve this sense of balance, until it feels right. Again, it is perceptual.

Balance, the location of the fulcrum point, can be along any axis. Axis refers to the demarcation between two halves of a symmetrical arrangement. Think of the axis as the crease line when we fold a piece of paper. The fold can occur along the horizontal, the vertical, or the diagonal. In each instance, there will be two halves of equal relationship and proportion to each other. When we introduce objects into these two halves, there will be a sense of balance or imbalance between them. The upper right portion of the screen can be in balance with the lower left portion of the screen. The downstage left area of the stage can be balanced with the upstage right area. In cubic space, the volume of that space can be broken up to a variety of axes: front to back, top to bottom, left to right. This creates a wide range of options for establishing balance or imbalance along a range of axes.

Proportion is the relationship between various objects, their relative size and weight, and so their importance or dominance visually. A sense of balance is created by the appropriate relationship of objects to each other. They will seem of similar sizes and shapes and their collective relationship will be inferred. They will seem to be part of a group. When objects are grouped in a disproportionate relationship to each other, there is a disjunction. The objects do not seem to be related to each other.

When discussing relationships between objects it is helpful to understand some of the principles of active and passive. When objects are grouped by even sets of numbers, as in two, four, and six, the perception of balance is between those objects. That is, the fulcrum point is along an axis line not connected to the objects. It is between them. When objects are grouped by odd sets of numbers, as in three or five, the perception of balance includes one of those objects. The fulcrum point is along an axis through one of the objects. The object actually becomes part of the balancing act. This more active engagement leads to a more active connotative value. Odd numbers of objects are visually more active than even numbers of objects.

Properties of Balance and Proportion

As noted before, balance and proportion relate to conditions of the physical world and our relationship to it. When standing and involved in activity, we are always engaged in the act of balancing ourselves and we relate to objects in terms of their distance from us. There is an intimate sensibility about balance. As a design element, then, balance is perceptual and intuitive. If design elements seem balanced (objects, color, line, texture), there is a sense of calm, harmony, security, and assurance. If design elements are out of balance, their relationship elicits feelings of insecurity and apprehension, a change from the calm. In context, this imbalance may be positive. It may be a feeling of dynamism and action, of activity. Something is about to change. If objects are proportionate to each other they evoke a feeling of stability and assurance. If they are disproportionate, they may evoke feelings of disjunction and insecurity.

Movement

Movement can be applied to a variety of design elements or combinations of elements. Movement is the apparent progression in a sequence of design elements. It is a recognizable order of repetition. We can look at an arrangement of objects and detect the sequence or order of the objects. We may begin to anticipate that order and predict the next logical movement, given the order we have just seen. A row of lines, for example, may suggest a continuation of that repetition beyond the objects we see. We begin to fill in where the movement leaves off. If the row of lines seems, by arrangement, to move across the horizon line, we can anticipate the continuation of that line along the horizon line. If three dots appear on one line, then five on the second line, then three again, we can anticipate a return to the five dot line next. Or we may see an arrangement of four vertical lines, then four lines on the diagonal, then four vertical lines again. We can anticipate the return to the four diagonal lines.

We begin to anticipate the arrangement of the objects from the clues we have been given. Our eye is being led not only by the repetition but also by the expectation of repetition.

Certain objects have specific and recognizable movement. An arrow is an example of an object with strong implied movement. The point of the arrow leads our eye to the direction in which the arrow is pointing. We can augment the effect by adding more arrows and strengthening the sense of movement. If all the arrows point to a bull's-eye, then the bull's-eye will be the logical point on which we focus. The arrows have led our eye to that point. Of course, certain compositions can lead our eye without the overt use of arrows. The actual composition in painting, for instance, can lead our eye to the subject or area of the painting the artist wants us to look at most carefully. The lines that lead us in this case are implied. Three sets of diagonal lines, implied by the drape of fabric or the bend of an arm, can lead our eye to the center point or the focus point just as easily as three arrows pointing out the direction to follow.

Properties of Movement

The sense of movement can occur in a variety of combinations of design elements. Line has already been discussed. The same principles would apply to arrangements of shapes or a particular sequence of textures. Moving through a particular range of hues or moving through a particular set of objects in sequentially different values of a color can also prompt the eye to follow that sequence. If a particular costume allocated the sequence of color shifts from top to bottom, this would encourage the viewer to move along the same path. The strategy in costume design may lead us to focus on the head or the heels of the character, dictated by the sense of movement in the sequence of color shifts.

This sense of movement can acquire rhythmic qualities. It can seem slow and ambling, or it can seem staccato and jittery. A crenellated parapet can suggest through the orderly arrangement of line a movement that invokes the sense of the military, or a Greek key ornamentation on a costume can suggest formality and rigidity. The random play of curving and intertwining lines can suggest something happy or frivolous while a repetition of strong bands of color on a sleeve can suggest something bound and regimented or orderly. As with texture, movement can take on added value when it is seen in large aggregates. An entire set can have implied movement through the various combinations of design elements. The costumes can have both individual and collective movement visually. Certainly the movement of lights (especially the lighting properties of direction and intensity) is a strong design element in the stage picture and can contribute substantially to the rhythmic context of the production.

Contrast and Variety

Contrast and variety can be applied to a range of design elements or combinations of elements. Contrast, as a design element, is usually a statement of difference. It compares two items by placing them together and showing their differences. We can, for instance, contrast one color with another. Blue can be contrasted with red. Or we can shift the value of the blue and have two contrasting shades of blue. Or we can contrast a deeper shade of blue with a lighter tint of blue. The shift draws attention to both the differences and the relatedness of the two colors. We can also contrast other design elements. A line moving in one direction can be contrasted with a line moving in another direction. Again the contrast between the two, the comparison, can draw attention to their differences and to their relatedness. A basket weave design is the contrast between horizontal and vertical lines. The same contrast applies to monk's cloth. We will look at the one square sitting in the middle of a row of circles because it contrasts with the circles. It is different. Our eye will be drawn to the one object in bright light in a darkened room. There is a contrast in intensity. Contrasts in texture can heighten the sense of the texture. A soft, velvety surface next to a concrete surface will accentuate both through the comparison. We are alerted to the differences by comparison.

Variety is usually a series of contrasts. It may be contrasts of like items or contrasts of dissimilar items. There can be a variety of colors in the design—contrasts between several colors together. There can be a variety of lines, shapes, and textures. There can also be variety between these categories of design elements. There can be visual variety established through line and shape or line and color or line and texture, for example.

Properties of Contrast and Variety

A simple shift in one line from a group of lines will draw attention to the different line. By its difference, it will draw the eye. Contrasts are a simple way of establishing focus. Contrast also alerts us to the difference between two design elements. This can be useful thematically, especially when we want to associate the contrast, or difference, in the design element with a group of characters or the shift in locale or mood.

Variety, like spices, will enliven. Variety keeps our attention and our interest. Things become less predictable. A simple black-and-white checkerboard will offer us contrasts in black and white. But by introducing gray squares, we begin to establish a variety, a range of color values that enliven the surface. A row of vertical lines will take on greater interest if the lines are of varying height. Our eye will move back and forth comparing the heights and their relationship to each other. Variety needs to be controlled, however, so that it does not become chaotic or too busy (lacking in focus) visually. Selecting carefully those elements that contribute to variety through subtle changes and contrasts will help keep a coherent visual sense.

Composition

It is the sense of composition, the use of the design elements together, that distinguishes the effective designer. Piecing together the "words"—the design elements—into a recognizable idea or sentence is the work of composition and becomes the objective of the good designer. Certain designers become familiar with the properties of certain elements over others. Their work becomes identified by this sense of emphasis, their vocabulary. Other designers learn to weave these elements together almost seamlessly in a way that we lose the sense of individuality. There is a sense of integration and comparability. Composition allows the viewer to take in the whole of the work, the canvas, as a total expression. Elements combine to create new combinations of information and aesthetic value. The canvas can be studied, literally as in painting, to discover the "canvas" applications for other visual design strategies. The canvas can then become the stage, the video screen, the three-dimensional event, the printed page, or the film.

Composition is the act of taking the individual elements and arranging them. Again, it is like the construction of a sentence, beginning with the words. Begin to train your eye as a grammarian. Look at the individual words and their arrangement. Locate the vocabulary and the syntax. How does the artist assign colors to various objects and shapes in the painting? How does light render the trunks of trees, their texture, in a wooded setting differently at twilight? What is the sense of balance between lines in the sculptural composition? What is the contrast in winter textures as opposed to summer textures in clothing? How does texture combine with shape to create new garden views? How do the steps of the courthouse combine horizontal line with vertical movement?

One great advantage in applying the principles of composition to other design areas is the shift in design elements from the two-dimensional to the three-dimensional. Instead of just looking at the canvas having width and length, we can now apply the principles to depth as well. Renaissance painters rediscovered this technique as a painterly illusion, called "forced perspective," but the stage offers us the real cubic volume, real depth, mobile depth. With the addition of depth, we can form new and shifting relationships between those elements. A different sense of balance can be created between downstage, center stage, and upstage. To the perception of left and right, up and down, we can add backward and forward as new movement options.

Training the Eye

At first trying to gain an understanding of so many variables in design may seem overwhelming. These design elements will become more familiar to you as you train your eye to look differently. You should begin by training yourself to break down the elements in your surroundings. Notice your environment, both the natural and the man-made. Try to isolate the particular design elements that constitute these environments. Look at clothing. Look out your window. Look across the street. Notice how design elements work collectively. Understanding this compositional quality to the design elements is the first task of the designer.

Notice the quality of light at different times of day and how design elements are constituents of that quality. Begin to explore, through books or actual visits, the museums that house painting and sculpture. Looking at painting allows us to look at how design elements have been manipulated and how they've been used by artists recognized for their skill and talent at this.

It is equally important to begin looking at the visual vocabularies of other cultures and historical times. Our own culture affords us one look at the world of design elements. There are other cultures that have found different combinations. And there are other times, historical periods, where the design elements have been used in very different ways, in different compositions. We can be stimulated as designers by recognizing these new or forgotten combinations of design elements and new "languages" of visual grammar. Good design cannot be parochial.

We don't want to get caught in the trap of thinking of this process as "precious." It is a survival skill. Visual arts have a very long history of using design elements and for that reason there is a lot of information. There is a lot we can learn from looking at visual artists who over the centuries have manipulated these design elements. We can look at palette—how artists have taken a select group of colors and used those colors to control the canvas—to control where we are looking and to define the relationships of the various parts of the canvas.

There are several artists like Rembrandt who have used palette to an extraordinary degree to suggest relationships between characters and events. Lighting designers for years have studied Rembrandt's rendering of light as a key dramatic element. Look at paintings. Look at sculpture. Notice how Rodin introduces texture to the process of sculpture or how Henry Moore uses shape in sculpture. Follow Louise Nevelson's use of shapes and forms and how she connects them with a neutral palette to create textural sculpture. Alexander Calder as a contemporary artist offers us real insights in the use of color, mass, and movement with his highly eclectic and energizing mobiles. The sense of playfulness in his circus sculptures can offer a whole world of information into the manipulation of line and how line determines form. Observe how Mondrian uses proportion and mass for a sense of balance.

One of the amazing things about the case studies at the end of this book is the number of people who go to museums and to exhibits. They speak of this without pretense and without artifice. It is a natural extension of their work, like reading the professional journals for other disciplines. A whole range of contemporary clothing designers pay periodic visits to New York's Metropolitan Museum of Art, in particular the costume collection, as a way of looking at fashion design in the past to find a source of inspiration for the present. They are not going there because someone told them it was good for them. They are going there because it improves the way they work. That means they are better designers.

2
Intentionality and Interiority: Finding Meaning in Design

Prospero: And—like the baseless fabric of this vision—
The cloud-capp'd towers, the gorgeous palaces,
The solemn temples, the great globe itself,
Yea, all which it inherit, shall dissolve,
And like this insubstantial pageant faded,
Leave not a rack behind.

from The Tempest
by William Shakespeare, Act Four, Scene One

I n the introduction, we talked about the sequence of responses a design might go through in creating a design idea. We then looked at the design elements a designer uses in creating a response. Now we need to look at ways to understand the intent of the writers and find strategies to augment that intent with our own visual devices, our designs. This intersection of design response, design elements, and the script or event is intentionality. To what purpose are we doing this project? What is the reason? Usually the answer resides somewhere within the intent of the author or the producer. Although it is important for designers to come to the script or the event with clear ideas and suggestions, it is the guidance and insight of the director and the producers that will determine the course of interpretation. Again, as Edward Albee suggests: "Learn how to see and hear a play, then realize it."[1] This chapter then is about how to read the text, how to translate that reading into a response and how to use the design elements in encoding meaning. As before, we will look at the process of theatre design as a template for other design strategies.

---

[1] Edward Albee, "Re: Interview," Correspondence with the author, 8, July, 2002.

Art and design are about making the artificial meaningful, and several questions need to be answered if we are to arrive at a statement of intentionality. Prospero alludes, in the *Tempest* quote that begins this chapter, to the insubstantial nature of the theatre, the sense of illusion that forms the basis of the event. By inference and inversion, he is also suggesting the theatre is a forum where substantial visions take place; vision supported by substance. The substance is the intention of the playwright, the author. Why did someone write this play? What was the point? What was the playwright trying to say? Is there some way in which we are supposed to change our thinking? Should we go out and do something? What did the playwright intend for us to think or do? Arriving at some sense of intentionality will then lead us to the interior of the play.

Think of the play as a house. The house has an exterior and an interior. The exterior can be cataloged with some degree of simplicity. It might be in the Tudor style, a bungalow, or a California ranch. It might be a two-story house or hang precipitously cantilevered over a cliff. It has windows that hint at the inside activity. It has a general shape and configuration with wings and porches and entrances. There is some hint of the character of the owners or those who live there but it is only when we go inside that the true nature of the inhabitants is often revealed. This is the play's interiority. This is when we begin to ferret out the intentions of the author. The inside of the house has the details of the occupants, what they like or what they seem to need. It suggests what they cherish or how they see themselves. There might be a cane or walker in the corner. What does that hint at? There might be very lacy curtains at the windows. There might be scattered messes or an imposing black leather sofa. The floor might be strewn with large lounging pillows and musician posters on the wall. There might be a fireplace with a mantel full of children's pictures. All these interior details suggest some aspects of the inhabitants. Although the exterior is the largest statement the house makes, it is the inside of the house that offers us clues to the real occupants. The interior of the house has several rooms, each of which has a different look and a different function.

In the same way, the script is the exterior of the house. It is the largest statement of intent. But once we move inside the house, we begin to find details and approaches, the implications and inferences of the script, that define the functions of the house more specifically and that add detail to the intentionality. Once we begin to analyze the script we are entering the rooms of the house and investigating their relationship to the exterior. We can think of this analysis as having two stages: a precognitive response where we intuit ideas of connotative value (for example, this play is dark and brooding; this play is like a maelstrom; this script is light and circular) and a cognitive response where our interpretations of the playwright's intent and the play's themes mediate our design choices. Again, this is where we encode meaning into our responses as designers.

If we are to explore this house successfully in the search for meaning and for intention, we need to become familiar with the rooms of the house and their purposes. Aristotle, the fourth-century B.C. Greek writer and philosopher, has helped us here by breaking down the dramatic event into six key elements:

Plot

Character

Theme

Dialogue

Mood

Spectacle

We can organize the first three—plot, character, and theme—into elements that form the structure of the play. We can define dialogue, mood, and spectacle as elements that contribute to the quality of the play, its tone. By looking at each of these structural elements and by determining their relationship to the themes of the work, we can begin to get clues that will help us determine those design elements, in combinations, that best reflect those structural elements. We can, as designers, support the intent of the author and bring new information to the themes and ideas.

The designer should ask about the structure of the plot, that is, the organization of the events of the play. What is the arrangement of the incidents? Usually there will be a beginning, a middle, and an end. There will be a story. Does the sequence of events suggest a specific kind of conflict? Can design help support that sequence, articulate the progressions, and delineate the shifts? Action, the activity of the play that emerges out of such conflict, can be of various kinds. It can be historical, emotional, intellectual, or psychological. It can be grounded in individual action or group action. Can design help distinguish that relationship? Can design clarify the individual action from the group action? The plot can be straightforward and linear. It can be convoluted and internecine. It can be full of turns and complications or simple and unpretentious. Where is the action of the play located? Does it shift? Is there a time factor in the plot and the action? How do we differentiate the changes in locale and time? Designers should evaluate the plot and the action so those elements can be reinforced and enhanced.

Character is another important script element. Designers will need to define characters in terms of social status, economic status, work status, emotional status, psychological status, and relationships to other characters, seasons, and locale. How do they talk? What kinds of words do they use? Are there clues as to how they might dress? Do they have a different way of talking? How do they react to situations? Do they express themselves clearly or covertly? Is their intent honest or deceptive? What is their objective—that is, what does the character want in the play?

The good designer will pay particular attention to the themes of the play. Does the plot or action suggest moral or ethical questions? Does the situation of the characters, where they begin and where they conclude within the time of the play, compare to situations at the time of the play's writing? Do those situations have relevance for our time? Is the play serious and of real gravity? Is it sarcastic and caustic? Is it lighthearted and frivolous? Is it funny and insightful? Are the themes personal, interpersonal, familial, historical, national, global, or cosmic?

If we go back for a moment to the analogy of the script as a house, remember we looked at the interior of the house as a life complete and perhaps different from the exterior. We can also say that the lives of the people in the house are reflective of themes that are personal and interactive. But the members of the household also have other relationships. They belong to a community, a region, a state, and a nation. How they are living out their lives could reflect on these larger associations. Maybe there is an even larger association that is global or universal. Themes can be personal, communal, and universal, even at the same time. In these terms, a script can have a theme that has a personal dimension, and at the same time has a larger dimension or importance that is communal in character or critique. The script can move further into universal themes that are not bound by region or specific personality but are recognized by many groups of people.

After looking at the basic structures of the work, the attentive designer will then turn to the qualities of the work: those elements that suggest the more elusive feeling of the work, the attitude and character of the discussion. Dialogue is a significant element in this search. What is the nature of the dialogue between characters? Is it realistic? Does it seem elevated and formal? Is it terse and sparse? Is it poetic? Does the dialogue have allusions to historical events and florid passions? Is there a lyricism to the language of the dialogue? Does the rhythm of the dialogue seem to move slowly, laconically? Or is it rapid-fire and staccato? Is it linear and straightforward or curving with starts, stops, and detours along the way? Is it cerebral and reflective or down home and spontaneous? Is it casual or formal? Is it witty or somber? Is it folksy or urbane? Is the dialogue circumlocutory? Is it psychological with interjections of "ums," "uhs," "aahs" and with room for extended pauses?

What do the combinations of elements so far suggest as to the mood of this work? Is it dark and foreboding? Is it philosophical and reflective? Is it grounded more in the action of the characters or their thoughts? Do the events seem to have gravity or are they light and spontaneous? Is it frivolous and happy? Is the mood reflective and pensive? Or is it bitter and cutting? Is the mood active and heart racing? Is the mood lighthearted and comical? Or is it dour and angry?

What is the sense of spectacle in this work? How is the attention of the viewer maintained? Is there an expansiveness and openness to the action? Do we have large events in large spaces? Is this a parade or a courtroom drama? Is there the sense of large movements of large groups of people? Or is this work intimate and domestic? Does the action occur in a kitchen between two people at a table?

It is also important to look at how the author describes these elements. How does the playwright describe the opening location? What adjectives are used? Can you detect an attitude at this point?

Look at the following two opening descriptions of locale for plays by two different authors. The first is *The Glass Menagerie* by Tennessee Williams.

Act I, Scene 1: The Wingfield apartment is in the rear of the building, one of those vast hive-like conglomerations of cellular living-units that flower as warty growths in over-crowded urban centers of lower middle-class population and are symptomatic of the impulse of this largest and fundamentally enslaved section of American society to avoid fluidity and differentiation and to exist and function as one interfused mass of automatism.

The apartment faces an alley and is entered by a fire-escape, a structure whose name is a touch of accidental poetic truth, for all of these huge buildings are always burning with the slow and implacable fires of human desperation. The fire-escape is included in the set—that is, the landing of it and steps descending from it. The scene is memory and is therefore nonrealistic. Memory takes a lot of poetic license. It omits some details; others are exaggerated, according to the emotional value of the articles it touches, for memory is seated predominantly in the heart. The interior is therefore rather dim and poetic.[2]

The second is *Waiting for Godot* by Samuel Beckett.

Act I: A country road. A tree. Evening.[3]

What did you imagine when you read these two descriptions? Did you see the location? Did you image a space, an emotion or a psychological sense? The Williams description is very detailed. Did this help or hinder your? The Beckett description is very sparse. Did this help or hinder you?

The playwrights for these two plays offer us completely different ways of thinking about the scene, the space in which the play will unfold. The Williams script is filled with poetic imagery and begins to link the set to the thematic issues that the play will explore. There is a sense of comparison and outrage, desperation and emotional angst. The playwright uses the opportunity to introduce a range of thoughts and ideas, not just a physical description. Conversely, the ideas cannot be separated from the description.

The Beckett description is no less effective, though considerably shorter. It is like haiku poetry, evocative and bare-boned. It too introduces an attitude, albeit considerably different from Williams. Beckett too begins to link the set to the thematic issues that the play will explore, but inferentially. Looking at how the playwrights describe their environments offers some first clues to intent. This can begin the process of what Clive Barnes, former theatre critic for the *New York Times*, offered as a challenge: "To stage a classic is an easy thing but to restore that classic to the hands, minds and blood of its creator is in itself an act of creativity."[4]

---

[2] Tennessee Williams, *The Glass Menagerie*, (New York: New Directions Publishing, 1987 by The University of the South and Edwin D. Williams) 27.
[3] Samuel Beckett, *Waiting for Godot*, (New York: Grove/Atlantic, 1982) 6.
[4] Clive Barnes, "Stage: A 'Cherry Orchard' That Celebrates Genius," *The New York Times*: February 18, 1977) C3.

How does the author describe the entrances and exits of characters? How does the playwright describe the attitudes and emotions as parentheticals before the actual lines (for example, Character A: (bitterly) No, I won't!)? How does the playwright describe the actions of the characters (for example, Character A enters the room hesitantly)?

Searching for the answers to these multiple questions is like finding pieces of a puzzle. We might compare this to the creative and scientific process known as *anastylosis*. Taken from the disciplines of architecture and archeology, anastylosis names the process of dismantling a structure stone by stone, in order to reassemble it more accurately. We can apply the same process to our analysis of the script. Our approach can be *anastylotic*. If we take the script apart piece by piece, area by area, and then reassemble it from our refreshed perspective, we can give it new life and new meaning. At first the individual pieces may not seem to have a relationship to the overall story or the other pieces. But once fitted together they become a larger picture. They begin to cohere and find their relationship to each other. Ask yourself, "Is the situation of this character similar to one in my own life?" "Is the character going through something similar to what I've gone through?" "Is the circumstance of these characters similar to one I've known in my own life?"

The answers may not be so personal. It may be that you see parallels in the script to other people around you or circumstances in your community or the nation. Perhaps the parallels are in the way you think. What is right and what is wrong? What is your responsibility? Perhaps the answers are in the sense of membership you have in a group, a community, the nation, or the world. Perhaps the information is religious and bears on your relationship to a higher consciousness. Trying to find the larger context for the play will help you move closer to the author's own position in writing the piece and to the significance of the work as an artifact within a cultural context.

Reading the script

Read the script, for the first time, in one sitting. This is an important first introduction and you want to give it your full attention. It is like meeting a new friend. You want to be able to concentrate and focus on the details. You also want to experience the script just as the audience will in performance. If you have to take a break, do so when there is one in the script, the division between acts or an intermission. This first reading of the script is important for first impressions. What is the mood of this piece? How is the script divided? If into acts, what are the differences between them? Are there differences of time? Are there differences of locale? Does the setting change? You may want to jot down some notes as you read to help you remember specific impressions or questions, but let the first reading be a careful introduction. Let the characters play out their lives in that little stage in your head. Imagine the locations and the room or the view. Let this first reading be with as little interruption as possible.

You want to get a sense of the characters talking in your head and to detect the rhythm, the movement and flow of events and dialogue. You want to be able to listen to the characters carefully, for the first time. You will want to have a quiet conversation with the play. Just as we were careful when first introduced to that new friend, we want to be especially alert to each character—to the nuances of voice, expression, apparent need or motive. How do the characters talk? What words do they use? What do they say about where they have been? What do they explain about what they are thinking or feeling? What is their rhythm? What is the sense of rhythm between characters and what they are saying? How is the play as a whole progressing? What is the sense of unfolding in the events of the play?

You will read the play many times. Each new introduction will offer new details and new perspectives. You may find things that went unnoticed the first time. A different logic to the organization of the script may emerge. A second reading of the play is more surgical. You are being careful and specific. Look for the differences in the division of the script. How are the acts different? How do the scenes shift? Use this second reading to dissect the structure of the play and its organizational strategy. You will take more notes this time.

Subsequent readings of the play can now be for particular purposes. How does the playwright describe the setting? How are the stage directions written? Are there special notes or explanations the playwright offers? You may read the script for character relationships. For complex scripts it may help to make a chart that is near you during the reading. Locate each character and their relationship to the other characters. If they are family members, what is their relationship? You can refer to this chart as a way of keeping characters separated during these first few readings.

You may want to keep a list of the locale shifts, or the minor changes to the locale such as time of day or how one part of the room becomes more important than another. These early readings of the script, with directed purpose, can offer very useful information and focus your attention to specific design issues. Final readings of the script may be very technical. How long do you have to do that costume change between acts? Can that castered platform be rolled on between scenes easily? How will it affect the rhythm of the play that you had noticed earlier? Does the audience need to know what is on the other side of that door? Does it make sense to cue the lights with a real time shift of sunlight or should each scene be in different light?

Dramaturgy

Sometimes the analysis of the script with all the categories and details just cited could be further augmented. Looking at the play's history, at the context in which it was written, a process sometimes referred to as "dramaturgy," can elicit even more information. If we know what was going on when the playwright was living (and where) and what others were writing and thinking, we might infer certain things about influences and reflections in the writing. Knowing when a work was written can also give us a time period in which to relate the play. This relationship may be literal, in that we may attempt to reproduce the period of the play. An example of this would be the historically accurate productions of the Greek dramas, Shakespeare, or Restoration drama.

In this approach to design, we would look to the extant information available about the time of the play and when it was written. We would then reproduce that time period in the designs. Or the relationship may be more informational. We may choose to update the location or the time of the play, giving it a contemporary edge or sensibility. But by acquiring the dramaturgical information about the playwright and the play, we will always increase our body of information and make our choices that much more informed and resonant with the text.

If there is a body of work for this writer, it might be useful to look at the other writing the author has done. This can be called the "author's oeuvre." The larger body of work will suggest consistencies of style and approach, ways of writing and organizing ideas, and patterns of thematics and characterization.

The relationship between the play as an extant cultural artifact and the context in which it was written is one of our most important tools as designers. By inferring the connections between the world of the writer and those events and thinking around the writer, we begin to get inside the writer's head, to think as the writer may have thought. This may give us a more intimate and grounded perspective on the reason the writer was compelled to create the work—the author's intention.

This research into the context of the script will offer up a whole world of details and information that can inform the choices we have to make as designers. Were there zippers in this period? Did people use napkins? Were there electrical lights? Which way did doors swing? How were rooms heated? These questions will begin to be answered through this careful gathering process. The designer does not always know the value of a particular piece of dramaturgical information but cannot discount the possible usefulness, in the broadest sense, of acquiring a more intimate sense of the writer's world and therefore, by extension, the world of the play.

Where do you find this information? Contemporary plays will offer a wider range of choices because we have more extensive documentation. We can look at videos of the area, the locale. We can find magazines that document the context of the play. We can read novels that parallel the time of the play. We can look through photography books that document the art, the everyday life, or the architecture of the locale. We can examine photojournalism magazines, newspapers, fashion magazines, and social history texts. We can use the Internet to locate a whole range of resources, including descriptions, photographs, books on interior design, and paintings. As the time period of the play recedes, the less information is available. The record also recedes. We may still have magazines and novels, especially first-person accounts. We may have movies from the period or newsreel footage. We may have manuals for construction or repair. We may have catalogs for new merchandise. And we still have old photographs. We can see what people wore and what the interiors of their homes looked like.

Earlier still we will have paintings and sketches. We will have written accounts and literary descriptions. We can look at photographs of the architecture of the period. The paintings can tell us something about the interiors of their homes and what they wore, but the divisions between socioeconomic classes will be more pronounced and the evidence less complete. We can see extant records of clothing in the museums and collections.

Earlier still, we can examine the tapestries and illuminated manuscripts as a record of life and activity. Frescoes and bas-relief in architecture can all offer clues. These earlier cultures will offer fewer details, though usually these are well documented and do not become as overwhelming or as difficult in choice making. Other, less well-documented cultures will be less accessible also but well worth the search. Anthropological texts, journals, narrative texts, and novels may offer clues to details and interpretations.

By filling in the details in the world of the play, you, as a designer, can begin to create an inventory of choices and possibilities. You can begin to suit the design element choices to resonate with the elements of the play in a way that is bolstering and supportive, perhaps even illuminating. Answers to these questions will suggest choices in line, color, shape, and texture. By applying the connotative values of those design elements, you can begin to create visual reinforcement for these analyses. Those design element choices, in turn, will suggest combinations of visual balance, contrast, variety, and visual movement with equal attention to connotative values. By using the script as the touchstone, the reference point in your decision-making process, you will begin to create designs that are closer to the intent of the author and more resonant with the play's interiority.

3
Application

Prospero: Now does my project gather to a head.
My charms crack not; my spirits obey; and time
Goes upright with his carriage.

from The Tempest
by William Shakespeare, Act Five, Scene One

aving investigated the range of design elements and having explored some of the ways to establish meaning in the script, we
can now pull these aspects of design together into an application. How can we translate our knowledge of design elements, in all
their range of combinations, into a coherent and recognizable design that resonates with the author's intent? Again, we will turn to
the work of the theatre as a model for our investigations. For this
chapter we will look at three design areas—set, costumes, and
lights—as our template.

How can we apply those individual design elements to specific
design areas? The thoughtful application of design elements takes
into consideration their connotative values. Remember that design elements can have emotional values, psychological values, cognitive
values, and aesthetic values. We have figured out something about
the puzzle pieces individually. We have learned about the "why" of
the puzzle, something about its intentionality and its interiority, why
it was made. We are now beginning to put the puzzle together. We
have begun the momentum that Prospero alludes to, in the quote at
the beginning of this chapter, when he says, "Now does my project
gather to a head." This chapter will offer suggestions about ways to
employ the design elements specifically. Hopefully these illustrations
will prompt your thinking about other areas and other combinations.

Color

We can begin by looking at color in costumes. We have already discussed some possibilities for color in our earlier discussion of this

design element. Those included color-coding and the use of a palette as an organizing device. Remember that color can be used in costumes to distinguish one character or one set of characters from another. We used the example of *Romeo and Juliet*, noting how color could distinguish the two families in that play. We can also use the controlled introduction of color into the costumes as a way of signaling shifts in the state or condition of the character. Here we used the example of Lady Macbeth and noted how the introduction of red into the costume, over the course of the play, could help suggest the shifts in her mental state.

Palette, too, is a way of bringing a coherent sense of the stage picture to the production. Rather than using random colors, we can control the range (their hue, their intensity, and their value) as a select group. We can create a whole range of colors, without losing the individual actors, by introducing variations of intensity and value to the selected palette. Color can be used to focus the attention on a particular part of the actor's body, also. We may want to emphasize the head or the hands or the waist, for example. By introducing contrasts in color at these areas, we can shift the attention of the audience, at least during the first introduction of the character in that costume.

Does the script move us through an emotional range? Do we start feeling one way with the play and then move to another feeling by the end? Does the locale reflect the state of being of the characters? If so, we can use color to distinguish those emotional shifts, character intent, and states of being. Can we use the connotative values of color to clarify the emotional landscape of the individual characters or as a group? We may want to create a progression of palette from the first act to the final act. This could suggest aspects of the narrative or plot. We may begin with a bright, sun-filled palette and progress to a somber, grayed-out palette. Or we could do the opposite.

Color in light can make a significant change to the stage picture. Shifts in color, especially washes (a general distribution of light across the stage), can change the whole character of the stage picture. We can move from a light and cheerful space to one that is ominous and threatening or sickly. We can use color to suggest the time of day (warmer colors for morning or evening and lighter colors for midday). We can use color to accent objects or people onstage and suggest offstage events. A fire offstage can be suggested by accenting the actors and objects with saturated colors from that offstage location, for example. Accents of stronger, cooler colors can suggest the play of color in a natural setting, such as dappled light through trees or the reflections of light off water.

Line

We can introduce line into costumes through surface details, fabric patterns, and the total silhouette. Surface details could include piping that creates bands or circles around arms, neck, and hems or sleeves. Period costumes can allow us to introduce ribbons, pleats, fastening details, cuffs, and ruffles. Again, we can use the connotative values of line to suggest certain character traits or states of being. By altering the total outline of the character in costume, the silhouette, we can also create line statements just as we noticed them in the line of trees on the street. Characters can become very vertical in appearance or very asymmetrical.

Line can be introduced into sets with surface details such as moldings, wall ornaments, or the implied line from architectural details such as a row of windows or a series of doors. Line can also be perceived as the aggregate of a whole range of shapes that, collectively, suggest a strong vertical or horizontal or diagonal character. Again, the connotative value of these statements can augment the intent of the production.

In lighting, line can be suggested by the perception of the beam throw of a particular lighting instrument or a combination of instruments. A row of strong down lights, parallel to the proscenium, can suggest a strong vertical. Or a series of strong down lights can create a diagonal line that slashes across the stage. A row of horizontal, floor-mounted up-focused instruments can again suggest a strong vertical line. The introduction of diffusion or fog media will accentuate these line statements.

Shape

Shape has a particularly strong application in costume design. If we think of the total silhouette of the actor in costume as a shape, we can begin to manipulate that shape in ways that contribute to our understanding of the character or the situation. Triangular shapes can create broad shoulders and cinched waists. Boxy shapes, like rectangles and cubes, can suggest a different silhouette, perhaps one more powerful. Spheres and ovals will allow for feelings of happiness or indulgence (as in gluttony). Period costumes are an opportunity to introduce even more exaggerated silhouettes and therefore more exaggerated shapes.

Shape is equally important in set design. It is here that major statements can be made using the connotative values of shapes. Large boxy cubes or rectangles will create very different masses than pyramidal and trapezoidal shapes, with equally different implications. Remember, too, that shapes can be perceived by the aggregate mass of the individual shapes. A pyramid of spheres will reflect taking one shape and creating a wholly new shape by the arrangement.

Lighting can be very important in rendering particular shapes onstage. Shapes can become flattened or their dimensionality exaggerated or emphasized. By shifting the dominant direction of the light, shapes can acquire different qualities and characteristics. They can lose depth or become exaggerated, even threatening. They can acquire shadows and shift their relationship, one to the other.

Texture

Texture is an important design element that is seen in each of the design areas. In costume design, texture can be the individual weave or finish of a fabric. The surface of burlap will have a different texture than satin or brocade. Furs and leather will have a different texture from metals and plastics. The way in which the fabric is gathered or arranged can create the texture (pleats, drapes, folds). A long cape with deep folds or a box-pleated shirt will register as different textural surfaces. The surface of the fabric can be ornamented with beading or piping, embroidery or feathers to create new texture combinations. Texture can be the layering of several fabrics on the same costume where both the volume and the edges contribute to a new surface feeling.

Texture in set design can be stated by the introduction of actual textural media onto the surfaces of the set (sawdust mixed with paint, spray foam, crushed paper) or by painting the semblance of texture (wood graining, marbling, spattering, or rag rolling). Texture can be the aggregate effect of several different surfaces on the stage. For example, an arrangement of cubes and rectangles can produce a range of angles and intersections. The quality of this intersection can have a textural quality. Swags and large drapes of fabric can create a different textural quality, particularly useful when combined with contrasting textures. Large masses of surface on the stage can also be broken up and given textural qualities. The surface can be hard and metallic or stuccoed and pebbly. It can be woven grasses and bark or polished marble and bronze medallions. It can be rough-hewn stones or it can suggest the metal tracery of scaffolding or construction beams. The surface can be treated totally to create a textured mass or the surface can be ornamented in some way to create a textural quality that breaks up the mass. Arrangements of pictures, wooden planking, openings, and framing can all give new textural statements.

We can also look at the intersection of surfaces: horizontal floors meeting vertical walls, sleeves meeting tunic at the shoulder point, or the shadow of a tree crossing the stone wall. All of these intersections can be seen in several ways that might contribute more information. Smooth, clear intersections suggest newness and a kind of blank page on which history has not yet been written. But when people live in spaces, when group activity occurs, that activity creates a record. The detritus builds up from use. Things get piled up. What may have started out as clean and sharp intersections of planes, over time and with use begin to acquire buildups. They become accreted intersections. Like dust buildups, these accretions soften the edges and pull surfaces into a stronger visual harmony and relationship. They also represent a kind of biography of space, of occupation. This can give spaces and surfaces a visual history with connotative value. Rooms can be read in terms of their occupants or mood or psychology. There may be piles of magazines near the fireplace, a basket of laundry near the door, piles of toys in the corner. The end of the bed may be littered with suitcases or books. A dress may be adorned with brooches, or have rips and tears or patches, or a shawl is added or an overcoat. The walls may be assaulted with neon flashes from an outside sign or the soft glow from a bedside lamp, or light can be filtered by a Venetian blind. All of these accretions soften the edges and intersections of walls and floors, of planar surfaces. They give the volume new texture and depth and add visual interest as well as information. Our lives are filled with these accretions, and we are accustomed to sorting through them visually and extracting information about the occupants and the activity.

In lighting, the most dominant suggestion of texture is through the use of patterned light. By using templates in the lighting instruments that create patterns, we can suggest a whole range of textures that are layered on the set and costumes. We can suggest light filtering through trees, scattered leaves on the ground, water and waves, or just a breakup of the surface into more abstract patterns of light and shade, sharp and soft edges, and variations in color that create variations in depth.

Balance and Proportion

Balance and proportion play useful roles in costume design as we have mentioned already in our discussion of silhouette. By emphasizing certain parts of the body or what the body carries at that point, we create areas of visual weight or importance. We may create a state of balance between the upper and lower torso or we may create a sense of imbalance between those two areas. We may exaggerate the proportional relationship between areas of the body and thus begin to comment on the importance of those areas. This can, again, begin to comment on aspects of character or the character's state of being.

Sets are among the strongest design areas in terms of balance and proportion. The sense of balance to the stage—either left to right, top to bottom, front to back, or across some diagonal axis—will be strongly inferred or implied by the mass of the set pieces and their arrangement. The connotative values of an implied sense of balance to the set will have an important and ongoing effect on the viewer. Because the action of a play often moves from one state to another, it is useful to create a state of balance in the stage picture that allows for uncompromised attention on the part of the audience. Although the picture can be shifted for important moments of transition in the plot, focusing our attention on the changes in weight and value, these shifts should be seen as exceptions.

Balance and proportion are also important factors in lighting design. The sense of balanced coverage on the stage or the significant lack of coverage in certain areas will contribute to a sense of balance and focus or some imbalance in the stage picture. Shifts in the direction of the light will shift that balance and contribute to the audience's sense of a shift in time (as with the movement of the sun) or ambience (a gathering storm) or imply other shifts such as emotional state, mood, or psychology. A turn of events can be signaled by the shifts of balance in the lighting. Shifts in the balance or intensity can also signal other changes for the audience. Certain areas of the stage become more important (an area of the stage with more light gets more of our attention), certain acts acquire different moods (one act can be darker than another), and certain characters can have their connection to other characters change (as they lose or gain light in relationship to the other characters).

Movement

Remember that movement in design terms is usually the implication, the suggestion, of movement. Actual movements, as with actors crossing the stage or drapes blowing in the window, are different forms of movement with equal and powerful implications. A large cape that commandingly opens up and moves powerfully across the stage is one kind of movement. A double set of skirt ruffles can flounce with another kind of movement. The silky scarf can echo the actor's movement and add new qualities to that movement. A long sleeve can repeat the hand gesture of the actor in a reflective movement. Larger masses of fabric, depending on their weight and weave, can also suggest movement patterns as the actors' movement energizes them. Designers can use the sense of movement in costume to signal several character qualities. There is also the implication of movement that can be suggested by costume details such as surface ornamentation, appliqué, weave, or patterns.

Movement in the set can be literal, as with wagons and platforms moving across the stage, shifting the scene. Scenery that is flown in and out creates a pattern of movement. Even the act curtain that rises and falls establishes a movement pattern before and after the play. Such movement can contribute to the qualities of the play in terms of tempo and style of movement. Such movement can be slow, unobtrusive, and mechanical or staccato, energized, and intrusive. There is a whole range of movement between those two also.

The movement can also be implied by such things as surface ornamentation, silhouette, the combination of shapes on stage, and how the outline of those shapes creates a pattern of movement. The set can introduce movement in how it is negotiated by the actors. Long entrance ramps (shift in height with long linear movement), stairs (shift in height with staccato or stately movement), and shifts in platform height will introduce actor movement that can translate to the style of movement for the whole play.

Movement is one of the most important aspects of lighting design. We sense the shifts in intensity of the instruments as a pattern of movement. Lights come up. Lights go down. Something starts. Something stops. The stage can become dim or intense. We also sense the shifts in coverage across the stage as movement. One area of the stage will get all the light or an area of the stage will get less light. These shifts in distribution will have a timed execution and that action will create a sense of movement. There will be movement in the sense of progression through the various cues and levels of the light. We also sense the shifts in intensity among various objects onstage as movement. In addition to shifting the direction of lighting, this area of design offers the possibility for shifts in intensity. Certain objects (and certain actors) can become brighter or certain areas of the stage can become brighter. These can be perceived as movements.

Variety and Contrast

Contrasts in costume design can be seen in fabric, surface ornamentation, color, and the range of distribution of design elements between the characters. It may be important to distinguish the lead character from the chorus, and by shifting some design elements, for instance color, we can emphasize the lead character through that contrast. Variety is important for maintaining interest in the stage picture, and a range of contrasts in design elements will help contribute to that sustained interest. Contrasts can delineate both different groups of characters, allegiances, and status as well as shifts in relationship, emotional state, and physiological bearing. The contrast between the colors and shapes and line of a character's costume in the first act may be contrasted with a significant and noticeable shift in those design elements in the next act.

Variety and contrast can be employed in the set design also. There may be noticeable contrasts in the shapes of the set and the line of those shapes or the ornamentation. Shifts in the texture of surfaces will accent those textures. Contrasts in color and shape can begin to suggest the movement of the play's plot or mood. The play of circles in contrast to sharp angles may suggest different tensions in the character's locale or mind-set. An important use of variety is in the treatment of the stage floor. By introducing ramps, rakes, steps, and shifts in platform height, the set designer can introduce a variety of heights for the movement of actors. This can have important value for the director in determining shifts in relationships, authority, and status. The sense of variety in levels can relieve the monotony of a single-plane acting space.

Lighting design offers several opportunities for contrast and variety. Shifts in intensity, color, direction, and coverage can create a range of visual stimuli. Variety is almost implicit in the execution of lighting cues. These may be subtle and beyond conscious detection or obvious to the audience. Scenes can be bright or contrastingly dim, softly lighted or harshly lighted. Colors in light can contrast warmth with coolness. The shifting direction of light offers a variety of illumination for the actors and the space, invoking a sense of the natural movement of daylight or the shifting forces on the characters and events. Lighting can offer contrasts in intensity too as a device to create focus on stage, to help determine where we will look. The brighter object will command our attention. We may shift from a fully lighted stage to a single spot on a lone character center stage.

Research

In addition to using the design elements in arriving at a design response for the text, we also need to support the application of those elements with another specific set of tools. These tools can be defined, broadly, as research. We already talked about dramaturgy, the historical research into the context in which the play was written. Now we can look at research that is specific to our design area. We have already looked at the design elements as having connotative value. Connotative value can also be inferred from historical research, and we can discover, as designers, ways in which previous cultures and time periods have established relationships between those same design elements. Research can be historical or contemporary, primary or secondary. The process is one of gathering information from a variety of sources that can help inform the decisions the designer has to make. This design research can be compared to the training an athlete may go through in anticipating a meet or competitive event. The training involves doing a series of exercises that anticipate the athlete being called upon to perform in a certain way. The exercise is not in and of itself an event; it is a preparation. The usefulness of research is, in the same way, in preparing the designer for some anticipated event. In this case the designer is preparing for those times when a decision must be made quickly and in keeping with the other decisions he has already made on a particular project. Research can lend a consistency of approach to a project and can create a context for decision making.

Research for design is sometimes referred to as "historical accuracy." By this we mean locating the design work in a particular historical period (for example, Egyptian, Elizabethan, the 1980s) and being faithful to that period's aesthetic and cultural values. We can determine the look of this period by research into the artifacts and records available that document that time period or culture. A costume designer, for example, will research the period and location of the play. The designer will then study the clothes worn in that period. The question of historical accuracy is, of course, a conceit. We will be looking at the historical period, not in terms of their ideals and aesthetics, but translated through our own.

In other words, we will be applying our sense of what looks good to what another culture or time period thought looked good. One need only look at the biblical film epics of the 1950s to discover that historical accuracy is subject to wide interpretation. It can be assumed that those designers were trying to be historically accurate, but the look of the costumes, the sense of what is important in the sets, and the kind of lighting all conspire to locate the work in 1950s America. Early photographs of stage productions of period plays convey the same betrayal of their own time.

But designers can still be afforded real opportunities for choices by locating the event, the script, in a time frame or period that reflects the intent of the author or the time in which the script was written. By immersing one's perspective in that of the author, the author's milieu, we can begin to get a feeling for the period and the look of the environment. The script is not an isolated document, somehow floating in time; it is, rather, a specific artifact of a specific period and resonates with or rebels against the thoughts and aspirations of that period.

To be historically accurate is to look at the cultural evidence that documents the period chosen for the script or out of which the script was written. Primary resources for this research are extant objects and information. Paintings, sculpture, architecture, clothing, jewelry, books, furniture, journal descriptions, and photographs— all are actual, extant evidence of that culture or time. Secondary resources have a filter imposed between the designer and the research. The evidence may be drawings of clothing of the period, for example. Another artist has interpreted the paintings, the architecture. Or the secondary source may be written descriptions. Or the evidence may be paintings of that period, but done in another period. Again, remember the example of the biblical film epics. Someone else has emphasized certain areas or design elements based on their own cultural bias. But primary resource is not always available to us, and as long as we investigate a range of secondary resources, we can move closer to an accurate interpretation of the period in question. Or we may be prompted to adopt an interpretation of that period by someone from another period.

This kind of design research can also be contemporary. Rather than looking at a period in the past, we are investigating a locale or culture less familiar than our own but existing in our own time frame. What is contemporary Russia like? We may think we know from some vague generalized images culled from recent news videos, but we would need to find other sources of visual information to fill in the missing pieces of information. What do the streetlights in Moscow's main square look like? When does it get dark in the winter? What are Muscovites wearing in the summer? How can we find that information?

The forms that this preparatory research can take are varied. We can look at paintings. We can read novels. We can look at photographs. We can look at art books. We can visit locations. We can listen to music. We can read repair manuals or old magazines. Good designers will begin to create their own inventory of resources, readily available research materials that can quickly inform them of certain periods or locales. The inventory is a survival tool. It can bolster our choices and it can prompt newer, perhaps more creative thinking. In all cases, we, as designers, are taking research information and using it to help us make decisions.

4
Style

Brutus: On such a full sea are we now afloat,
And we must take the current when it serves,
Or lose our ventures.

from Julius Caesar
by William Shakespeare, Act Four, Scene Three

Romeo: But He, that hath the steerage of my course,
Direct my sail!

from Romeo and Juliet
by William Shakespeare, Act One, Scene Four

Style is one of the most difficult categories of design to pin down. It is truly a "full sea" complete with swells, depth, volume, and constant changes. "Style" as a descriptive is used in many different ways and in all areas of design and production work. A play's staging may be called "stylish" by which we mean we are aware of its style and the currency of that choice. Style may also allude to a particular historical period (as in Elizabethan style) or a person (as in Chekhovian). Style may be architectural. There can be a Baroque style to the design, or Gothic or Art Deco.

Style can allude to a particular school of painting or individuals. There can be an impressionistic style to the design or the designs can be in the style of Picasso. To add to the confusion, using style as an organizing strategy for designers means responding, also, to the style of acting (for example, method, Kabuki, organic), the style of directing (for example, Brechtian, ensemble, realistic), and the style of writing (for example, presentational, episodic, fragmentary). But as Brutus advises, "we must take the current when it serves." We must find the style that serves the play and the play's meaning. And we must have someone or something to direct our sails.

Style can also be described as an attitude to the production. Style can be a series of choices in several elements of the production process that become a coherent guide or map for exploring the script or the event. Style can suggest, "Here is my take on this material. This is what I feel about it." In this sense it becomes the current that serves our efforts as the quote from the beginning of this chapter suggests. A production of *Julius Caesar*, for instance, might use riot police and video cameras as a way of contemporizing the themes of the Shakespearean drama for a modern urban audience. The style is appropriating other cultural symbols and is saying: "I think this material is relevant to us now. Let me show you some comparisons."

Style can refer to an attitude (as in cartoonish, lighthearted, and without gravity) or a period (as in Victorian). Sometimes it is both. The Victorian style not only suggests a period (the reign of Queen Victoria, 1837–1901) but also an attitude (prudish, fussy, stuffy, formal) and interiors characterized by dark wood, heavy drapes, palms, somber colors, fussy decorations.

Style can be seen as an organizational strategy for the many questions and choices that can come up in production design. By using the template of a particular style, the various design areas can move toward a coherence, a kind of visual unity, that will help connect the elements. If the costume designs are resonant with the set design and the lighting design, then the production will acquire a sense of consistency of thought and intent that will help the audience to understand the production as a whole, rather than as separate or independent units, or different or even competing voices. If all design elements are coordinated under the imprimatur of a style choice, the production will gain strength in expression, one area will reinforce another, and we can get closer to the author's intent as a group effort.

Remember, however, that theatre is a human endeavor and therefore subject to the vagaries, creative revolts, and spontaneous connections that make the creative act unpredictable and alive. Think of style as a sliding scale. Various approaches to production design will move along this scale, sliding from or toward our willingness as an audience or participant to believe in the reality of what we see. Style is not a series of discrete cubicles in which we store and retrieve a particular style. It is a mobile, fluid process of choice-making in design. As designers our concern should be with the consistency of approach among the design areas and elements. The major design areas—costumes, set, and lights—need to agree to the same style. We can illustrate this scale as seen in Figure 4–1.

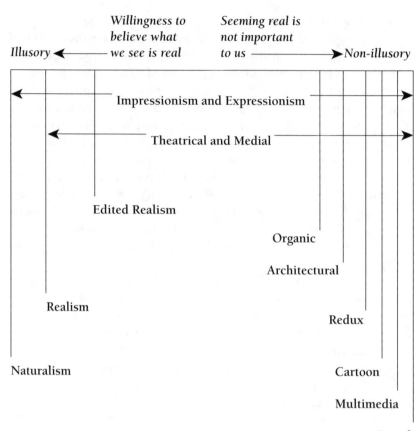

Figure 4–1

The most significant and organizing component of style is real-ism. Almost all styles are a movement toward or away from realism. For the purposes of our discussion we can refer to realism as a style of design that seems to replicate the natural world as we experience it.

Movements away from realism we can catalog, generally, as the-atrical or "medial." By theatrical, we mean styles that recognize the presence of the theatre and the theatrical event; by medial, we mean of or relating to the medium being used. Although theatre can be considered a medium, it has a whole lexicon of conventions and methods that are unique to the live event. Medial as a style, for the purposes of this discussion, will mean styles that invoke technolo-gies that interpose between the event and the audience. This would include television, film, video, and video games. Medial styles invoke the reality (again, technical) of the form in which they are presented. Neither of these styles attempts verisimilitude or truthfulness to our perceived physical world; instead, they invoke the sense of ritual or event without a suspension of disbelief on the part of the audience. We do not forget that we are at a parade or at the theatre or playing a video game if these presentations are within these styles, theatrical or medial.

The design elements for style can be broadly categorized into those combinations of elements that create an illusion of the real world and those that do not. Some designs are representational and re-creational; they try to represent, to recreate the natural world, as though what we are seeing or experiencing is like other experiences or sights in the natural world as we live it. This is realism. The tree looks like a real tree, like the one we played under as a kid. The train station looks like a real train station, like the one we have waited at. Film and television work are often centered in this style of design. Things appear as they "are." The other broad category of style is presentational. It does not hide the mechanisms of presentation. Theatrical and medial are in this category.

Realism

This style is sometimes called "the potato." Realism is supposed to be as honest and forthright as a potato; this is about our everyday lives. It began as a literary reaction to the emergence of the middle class as the primary theatregoer and to the development of psychoanalytical thought as another way of explaining human behavior. It was not about the aristocracy or the aspirations and intrigues of court life. Naturalism, a variant on this term, is sometimes called the "dirt on the potato." It takes realism one step further. Both are forms that try to replicate, to some degree, the real world, the world we see or the world we think we know. The conceit of these styles is undermined, of course, by the fact that the world is seen by each of us differently. But the determining factor in these two design styles is that the designs appear "real" by a generalized standard.

As mentioned, much of film and television design is based in realism. This is partially due to the connection between film and our knowledge of the camera. The camera (both the photographic camera and, later, the film camera) appears to us to record the world as we see it. If we take a photograph of a person at the beach and then print that picture, the scene is recognizable. There are elements in the photo that seem like the beach we remember when we snapped the picture. There does not seem to be an imposition of artistic license in the process. The camera "has not lied." No one seems to be interpreting the scene for us. As most photographers and photography critics have discovered, of course, there is a wide range of interpretation that goes on here. How the camera frames the object; what is left in or left out; how the background and foreground are related to the subject—these are all choices the photographer (or director of photography for film, video, and video games) has made. Digital manipulation of images will render the sense of verisimilitude (truthfulness to life) connected with photography increasingly suspect.

In spite of early and ongoing experiments with other styles for film and television, realism became the dominant style for film work early on and has remained consistently so. To some extent this is because the actors in these media are recorded in the same way as the scenery, and our tendency is to "interpret" their work as we would the stage actor. The film actor is not, however, a live presence. In film, if the actor appears real, then the scenery must also appear real to maintain a consistency of stimuli and accept the convention that the camera has recorded the "event" honestly. In other words, to make the actor appear more real, the design needs to be equally real. Although there is a wide range of choice making in film and television work, this dominant style dictates those choices.

Theatrical and Medial

We can catalog movements away from the style of realism, again, as theatrical or medial. They reference the theatrical event or the medium in which they are presented.

If we return for a moment to the comparison between our perceptions of the actor and our perceptions of the scenery, we can say the theatre offers us a real actor. We know the actor is real; we could reach out and touch her. No medium has been interposed between the work of the actor and us. Because of that reality, the scenery can move into a wider range of styles, away from realism, without compromising the realism of the actor. Theatricalism as a style is a combination of design elements, acting choices, and directorial intent that say, "This is a theatre, there is no pretense here and no need to pretend something is other than what you see." The style can be used to highlight the pleasure of the theatrical event, the pretense of the characters, or the implication of artifice and dishonesty. Brechtian style, a particular form of this theatricalism (alluding to the playwright and theorist Bertolt Brecht), often employs theatricalized elements to get the audience to think rationally and critically and to distance the audience from purely unexamined, reflexive emotional responses.

Video games have also enjoyed a less restrictive stylistic heritage. They come from a world of board games, comic books, and book illustration around myths so the freedoms allowed have so far generated more stylistic breadth. The early software also precluded much detail work so realism was not an option. Cartooning as a style was more accessible and could be rendered with the given technology at the time. Large, fairly flat planes of color and simple shapes and forms limited rendering of depth through the use of light, shade, and shadow, or texture created a simple, cartoonlike style. This early freedom has allowed for more stylistic latitude because the "characters" in the games are also rendered in the same manner as the scenery. The "style" of the rendered actor can be the same as that of the scenery. Each introduction of a more "realistic" actor into the games heightens the tension between the observed reality of the "actor" and the stylization of the "set."

Partial or edited realism (sometimes called *selected realism*) is a more conscious conceit. It allows for realism, but, as with the camera, selects those areas to be represented. We are not trying to create the whole world of the narrative as we think people would see it. We are selecting individual elements to represent that world. We have consciously made choices, in a studied way, for our view of the world of the narrative. For the stage, this could mean doing a cutaway of the interior of the house but without all the walls and lawn and neighbor's fences. Jo Mielziner in his theatrical design for Arthur Miller's *Death of a Salesman*, offered us the barest outline of a house, a skeletal framing at best, but set each room of the house with partially real walls, real chairs, and real tables. The world we see through the walls is not of neighbors but the world of commerce, the overpowering tenements and high walls, the fire escapes and ominous multistory facades of the cityscape.

Black box theatre, the popular architectural form for theatrical performances that often resulted from found spaces (such as storefronts) that were rectangular (the box) and painted black to drop out distractions like overhead pipes, conduit, and heating vents, uses this style to great effect. Similarly, theatres-in-the-round use this style as a way of quickly moving scenic pieces off and on the stage without the benefit of a curtain to hide the process from the view of the audience.

Impressionism and Expressionism

Impressionism and expressionism represent two of the most important and general styles of approaching the text after realism. Impressionism as a design option is a style similar to that mode of painting we call impressionism. Impression began as a term of derision and scorn by Parisian art critics directed toward a particular group of painters including Monet and Pisarro. Today, the term has come to identify one of the most collected, admired, and eagerly viewed styles of painting in any museum's collection. Of these two styles, impressionism came first in the middle to late nineteenth century, and roughly parallels the beginnings of photography. Expressionism came later in the early twentieth century, and found its most ardent following in Germany.

These two styles have great influence in the way designers approach material, either consciously or unconsciously. We can use the character of Laura in *The Glass Menagerie* to help us understand the differences between the two forms. In impressionism, we are trying, as designers, to represent to the audience the world we see Laura living in. It is our impression, as designers, of her world. We are not trying to make a documentary here. Every reality of her life is not represented. We are not trying to realistically portray the St. Louis of the 1940s. We want to give the audience a sense, mere suggestions, of what Laura's world might seem like. In performance work, it is the audience's perception of the eye of the designer and director as an attitude to the subject that characterizes this style. The eyes of the designer and director become part of the conscious interpretation. And the audience is often asked to fill in some of the details.

It is perhaps best described as a statement of how the artist is looking at the subject from the outside, the overall impression. If we look more subjectively at the script, the screenplay, or the game description, we can begin to say, "Through whose eyes do I want to see the events of this narrative?" This becomes, then, a subjective choice. It may be one of the main characters: for example, Laura.

Expressionism is best addressed as a polarity of impressionism though the distinctions can easily become academic. As a style of design, it becomes the total look of the product, the play, the movie, or the game. It is usually characterized by exaggeration, usually in color or line or shape or texture. Since all art is, to some degree, an expression of what we see or think, this can be a confusing term.

We may describe expressionism as the interior world of the subject being reported out by the painter or the artist. The environment transforms, like a metaphor, into the inner life of the character, especially the emotional and psychological life of the character. The classic example of expressionism, Edvard Munch's lithograph "The Scream," can help us understand expressionism. All the elements of the environment contribute to the sense of the person's anxiety and fear. The environment becomes transmogrified by the subject's state of being. The artist is showing us the world of the screamer and how that world is like a scream. Since much expressionism predated (and therefore anticipated) World War I, this view of the world is especially chilling and emotionally charged. The sky echoes the shape of the mouth, the head, the fjord. The artist has incorporated his sense of the character into a view of the character's locale, the character's world.

With expressionism we, as designers, would be trying to represent Laura's inner life by designing her environment as she might see it. Here the choices we will make for her mother, Amanda, and her brother, Tom, in terms of the look of the room, the costumes, and the light plot may change because we are looking at them through a chosen perspective. Amanda does not see herself as her daughter sees her. Tom does not see himself as his sister sees him.

This same process can apply to the screenplay with the addition of the camera as one of the design choices (including point of view—where the camera assumes the "eye" of one of the characters rather than as an independent or omniscient observer). Taking this position is sometimes described by the question: "Whose play is this?" Though that tends to be an oversimplification, it can begin an important discussion of choices. The same can be said for the video game. There is a great deal of expressionism being employed, for example, in game design. Who is the game player? Are we seeing the world of the game through their eyes? Or is the game player being imposed in a world of outside order?

Much of design work can be cataloged in some way under the rubric of these three styles: realism, impressionism, and expressionism. But there are variations on these that offer a wider range of possibilities and organizational strategies. Some of these other styles have, again, borrowed on the lexicons of literature and visual arts.

Often the development of these performative styles was concurrent with that literature and those visual arts. Romanticism was clearly established as a literary and visual style and those definitions inform the designers' use of that style. Other styles adopted at one time or another include: classical, pop art, postmodernism, gothic, tribal, and experimental. Classical, or classicism, invokes those qualities believed to have been subscribed to by the Greeks. There is a presumption about the rigorous employment of the "unities" of time, place, and action. This usually translates into a visual style that invokes the classic fifth-century Greek civilization.

Pop art alludes to the movement in the middle to late 1960s of commodifying art into a product of consumerism and elevating everyday objects to artistic status (as in Andy Warhol's Campbell's soup cans). Postmodernism as a visual style alludes to the intent of the maker as a prime motive for the work. The role of the artist becomes apparent in the design. Gothic refers, again, to a specific historical period and is currently popular with video games because of the invocations of myth and Arthurian legend. Tribal as a style refers to cultural value systems and how those systems become represented visually. There is an invocation of cultural values that move away from western European and explore different or less familiar units of social construction and aesthetic value.

There is a style called "experimental" that admits to the laboratory status of the theatre. The audience becomes aware of the experimenting nature of the performance, the raising of questions about the event, and our participation in it, which form the organizational and design choices. There can be a liberating or self-conscious nature to this form depending on our openness to the experiment, our familiarity with the terms of the experiment, and our role as an audience in that experiment.

There is a style known as "cartooning" that uses the strong outlines and solid, primary fill-colors of comic strips and animated cartoons to dictate the look. This style has been used to suggest exaggeration, playfulness, or one-dimensionality. It can be ominous, as in Josef and Karel Čapek's dark and foreboding expressionist treatise *The Insect Comedy*, in the same way that a clown's face can suddenly move from happy to grotesque. Or the attitude can be childlike, playful, simple, and honest as often used in the Charles Schulz and Clark Gesner musical *You're a Good Man Charlie Brown*.

There is "organic" as a style that attempts to interpret the environment, especially one that is ordered or highly developed, through organic looks (especially earth tones) and textures as an irony or to make a comment on the more primal motivations and passions that underlie the urbane or civilized exterior. This seems particularly popular with Shakespeare. The use of strong vegetable-based textures and colors and natural forms such as tree bark, hemp, and sea grasses suggests the more "primal" emotions and conflicts beneath the apparently "civilized" exterior of the world of the characters.

Another style, popular at the moment, might be called "architectural." It takes from the performance space itself, deconstructing the idea of the proscenium as a framing of illusion and admitting to the theatrical space. It adopts the attitude: "This is a theatre and we are not trying to fool anyone." Eugene Lee used this to good effect in the design for the Broadway musical *Ragtime*, where he introduced architectural forms (the iron pillars of the now-destroyed New York Pennsylvania train station) as an allusion to a certain period and attitude in American history. He defined the space primarily with these shapes moving both inside and outside the proscenium arch.[1] This style echoes the very influential Russian theatre movement known as constructivist, characterized by a frank admittance to the "machine" of the theatre space, both its volume and the actors. Large flat planes of color, heightened angularity, extensive use of undisguised platforming, and exaggerated silhouettes in costume design all conspire to create an alienating effect on the viewer. Both examples invoke feelings of repression, economic control, and loss of individual freedoms.

Other styles may invoke the historical. Using production values from the original period of the script or the invocation of that period will result in a specific style choice. For example, we may produce a theatre piece in the wing-and-drop, painted scenery style of the 18th and 19th centuries. We may locate the game in the Gothic labyrinths of the medieval castles. We may have the camera follow the chase in the style of the Max Sennett Keystone Cops two-reeler silent film comedies. These are usually not slavish recreations of a historical period; rather, the period becomes a launching pad for fresher combinations of design elements associated with that period and results in more contemporary interpretations.

Some historical styles refer to specific people who defined certain looks in that period or were of the aristocracy that patronized

---

[1] Eugene Lee, "Re: Interview," Telephone conversation with the designer, 27, July, 2002.

it. We have period styles such as the English Queen Anne (especially in furniture), the French Louis XIV (also known as Baroque), and the more generalized period styles Directoire and Empire. There are period styles known by their furniture makers, including Chippendale, Hepplewhite, Sheraton, and Duncan Phyfe. We have clothing periods named for artists, such as Antoine Watteau (1684–1721), the French painter who focused on a fashionable and voluminous pleat beginning at the nape of the neck, now called the "Watteau pleat," but which came to characterize a whole period. Then, too, there is the famous simple black dress of Coco Chanel, which also characterized a whole period. In lighting there are notable periods such as the gaslight and limelight eras (roughly paralleling the Victorian era).

As with other historical styles, codifying the look is a matter of distancing—our ability to look back on a period of history and acquire something of a sense of objectivity. Once the period is over, reviewed in relationship to larger political, social, cultural, and economic events, the style becomes a defining look for that period and the period, in turn, becomes named by the style.

Another style of design has been cataloged generally as "multimedia." This style of design admits to the power of other media appropriated for theatrical purposes. Examples include productions using live cameras, monitors, television screens, slide projectors, LCD projection screens, biofeedback amplifiers, visual or aural amplification systems, hydraulics, and head mikes. Basically, this design concept allows for the introduction of other media technologies into the theatrical frame as one way of "updating" the experience. In the Broadway production of the musical *Rent*, characters wore clearly visible head mikes and they remained there regardless of whether the character was singing a solo or interacting with the other characters. The technologies and their presence onstage, as with the orchestra, became part of the design and part of the style.

Another style we might call "redux" invokes a past style but through a contemporary lens, a contemporary sensibility. We use the style and its historical period as a comment. This style takes our attitudes to one style and what it invokes and applies that style to a production as a way of making a comment. We are not merely trying to recreate that period or that style. We are trying to take our current attitudes to that style and apply them to the project and the designs. The fashion designer Mariano Fortuny used classic Greek drape and cut for his designs, thereby invoking an association with timelessness and museum chic. He was also active in theatre design but became famous for his proprietary methods of dying and pleating fabric. Other redux invocations might include the puritanical milieu of colonial America, the futuristic world of the cartooned Jetsons, the 1950s simplistic nationalism, the 1960s new-age freedom and innocence, or the 1990s sense of self-centeredness and financial excesses.

If we did a production of *The Tempest* and set it in a mythical or Woodstock-like setting, invoking the historical period of youthful rebellion in the America of the 1960s complete with tie-dyed shirts, flared pants, Indian print skirts, flower garlands for long hair, and music from the same period, we would be layering another level on the production. We would be asking the audience to use their attitude to the period of Woodstock as a lens for interpreting *The Tempest*.

Filmic styles that reference the filmmaking and video process (as with direct address to the camera) would be medial. A website that shows the workings of the navigational process would be medial. There are many variations on these themes, and each new generation of designers creates new permutations of design to address new ways of looking at the world or new expectations from the media.

Much of current style in design follows the breakdown of discrete categories in visual arts and literature. Because we have access to so much more information and history, these discrete categories no longer placate or comfort us, and the distinctions are much more permeable. We have a whole inventory of options. The sheer range of expression means that categorization becomes overwhelming and only the most general of terms can now be used, in their own way suggesting the melding of styles and the integration of their effect. The value of reference is now primarily as a method of collaborative process. The references are a way to communicate what we are thinking, using styles as a kind of shorthand for those discussions rather than as a template for all design decision making.

Style is, finally, about the how and why of something conceived. It is important that style be thought of as a coherency. Style should bind together the many elements into a coherence, a logic of choice making that allows the viewer to move smoothly and easily from image to idea to conclusions. The style of directing should be commensurate with the style of the scenery, the style of the costumes, and the style of the lighting. The acting style also needs to be consistent with these. The viewer will perceive this consistency as a unity of expression, a clarity of image and word. Inconsistencies in style will become jarring, disruptive, and even confusing to the viewer. The message and the information will become fuzzy or scattered. Style becomes the glue.

5
Design, Media, and Collaborative Process

Helena: *Whate'er the course, the end is the renown.*
from All's Well That Ends Well
by William Shakespeare, Act Four, Scene Four

Hamlet: *Our thoughts are ours, their ends none of our own.*
from Hamlet
by William Shakespeare, Act Three, Scene Two

In the introduction we talked about the process of design, the sequence of events with collaborators that leads to a design decision. In this chapter we are going to look at some of the dynamics that can influence that collaboration. Since the beginning of the twentieth century, design in the theatre has been a collaborative process. No doubt there were collaborators before this, just as there were designer and director-auteurs such as the seventeenth-century designer-producer-architect, Inigo Jones, the nineteenth-century producer-director, the Duke of Saxe-Meiningen, and in this country at the turn of the twentieth century, David Belasco. Each artist combined design with text in conscious and applied ways.

But the early twentieth century marks a particular point in theatre history for the emergence of the individual artists and individual design areas. Throughout the twentieth century, designers were acknowledged to have unique and specialized contributions and skills as artists who understood the collaborative nature of theatre making. They understood that the result of the collaboration was an "end, none of their own." It was not the individual act that was important, it was the collective act. With this came a sense of membership in an artistic and creative enterprise.

The idea of bringing specialized skills and talents to the process of theatre making and moving the design process above mere accessorizing or interior design elevates the design forms to a recognizable level of importance. To paraphrase, some are born artists, some become artists, and some have artistic expectations thrust upon them. Designers have become significant, making contributions on a level with the director and the playwright.

Moving away from the one-voice model, however, poses problems. Who speaks when? What is the hierarchy of decision making? How do ideas get shared? What strategies will help in the decision-making process when it involves more than one person?

Collaboration

One of the most critical skills a designer can have is the ability to collaborate. One of the areas for which designers are least trained is collaboration. Collaboration means a group of people working together for a common goal. In working together, these people need to find the ways to communicate their interests and opinions without scuttling the objective. Two skills can help ensure the objective: listening and preparation.

If the enterprise, the production of a theatrical work, is to benefit from the contributors, those persons need to feel their contributions are valid; that they have some latitude in the creative endeavor; and that their membership in the collective vision is important. Since the majority of the decision making will fall on the director and the producer, these two offices are critical to the sense of membership and the encouragement of new ideas and new ways of thinking about the project. We expect the director and the producer to have a vision. We expect the designers to respond to that leadership with intelligence, artistry, and ingenuity. If the leadership is lost, the endeavor is jeopardized. If the designers are not forthcoming or invested, the endeavor is jeopardized.

Collaboration involves meetings. Either the designer will meet individually with the director or with the director and the producer or with the whole team, including the other designers and specialty people (for example, hair and makeup, stunt riggers, choreographers, second units, fly riggers). Early meetings should, first, lay out the ground rules. The ground rules include who is in charge and responsible for what, what date something is due, how the group will stay in contact. If some areas requiring certain action overlap, whose jurisdiction will cover it?

These early meetings will also include exchanges of the process this particular group will go through. There are no set dynamics though there are boundaries for each participant. Each production will create a new set of expectations and a new group dynamic. Early meetings will help ensure the smooth running of this enterprise, regardless of the participants. As territories of responsibility are laid out, those who are responsible for assurance and checking will be identified. This is a "Who's in charge?" question, and although general categories of responsibility will usually be the same, it is always a good idea to reinforce and reiterate the hierarchy.

In addition to laying out the ground rules and explaining the process, the early meetings should define the group goals. This will usually include some discussion of intent, what the group hopes to achieve with this project, and some sense of an overriding, arching vision for the project. By explaining the way this particular group of artists will approach the text or the event, what the intent of the writer is, and what defining characteristics such as metaphor will be used, the group can find a common reference point for the myriad choices that will subsequently have to be made. Reiterating the goal, the vision for the project, throughout the process will help maintain a reference point for all participants.

Special emphasis should be placed on those areas of agreement in these early meetings. This will not only begin to solidify the group effort, the sense of membership and coherence, it will also begin to establish important feedback and encouragement for active participation. Just as with the process of mediation, this early collaborative process is a gathering of information, designing options from that information, and choosing the design options agreeable to all parties. The beginning stages of collaboration call for active listening skills, remaining alert and focused on the direction of discussions. Participants should get in the habit of restating what they've heard as a way of creating a consistent language among participants. This will help match intent to execution.

This is also an important stage to establish accountability. Each participant should feel some sense of obligation to full and timely execution of responsibilities. By reiterating the purpose, the vision, or the objective, participants can calibrate their contribution—that is, their time and effort—more effectively. By holding participants accountable at this early stage and by noting lapses, the group can help avoid the more difficult failings in expectation at a later, and more critical, stage.

A key to this process of gathering information, generating options, and choosing options is the perceived degree of investment. Each participant is expected to bring full membership and contribution to articulating problems, directly stating their interests and demonstrating enthusiasm for the group effort. Each participant should be perceived by the group as having genuine curiosity about the project, the possible solutions, new materials, and new approaches. Holding back at this point will signal less than full engagement and commitment and may lead to either having your ideas not listened to as carefully as you might hope or being dismissed outright. As a designer you need to find a level of enthusiasm for the project that you can share with the whole group. If you can't find some measure of enthusiasm for the project, then you probably should not be doing it.

The complexity of contemporary media and theatre work places collaborators in the awkward or rewarding circumstance of codependence. Directors cannot work without designers. Directors, however, cannot think for designers. Directors can only think with designers. The same is true of the producers. Trying to think like the other participants (what they are going through) will create a sense of group effort. Why is someone so anxious about the deadlines? Do they have a different sense of what can be accomplished? Have they had experiences where time ran out too soon? Why is this person so concerned about money all the time? Is it because they are running out of it? Why is this person pressuring for such early resolutions to design problems? Have they seen designs compromised without sufficient time?

Theatre is an organizational endeavor. It is constrained by a clear timeline. The production or event has a date for opening usually set and a time the audience will join in, also usually set. And there is never enough time. The collaborative nature of theatre has both cultural and historical frames. There is a succession of practitioners (directors, designers, actors, producers, and so on) who interact with each other within certain boundaries. These boundaries are identifiable by historical practice (who is responsible for what) and cultural context (who pays for what). This usually means that directors are responsible for the overall attitude, feel, and interpretation in a production; and constraints or prompts on that process are the province of the producers who too have a vision and an amount of money. Designers are responsible for an interpretation, a look and a style, executing and expanding on that larger vision and directive. When such boundaries are maintained, problems can be identified and solved. Traditional ways of doing things offer the comfort of convenient continuity where people can recognize each other's role and the process of collaboration is encouraged. Shifts from this organizational paradigm require new definitions of roles and new expectations of those roles. This does not mean that there are not other organizational strategies; it means that each organizational strategy has a range of consequences for each participant. In balancing the power of decision making it is important to determine whose voice is being heard and it is necessary to have an atmosphere of equality. It is equally important to determine who has the final voice.

Not all decisions will be made in large groups. Some decisions will be independent and some can be in smaller group units. Sometimes the smaller caucus will solve problems more easily and more directly. Sometimes, especially when conflicts arise, smaller group meetings can work out solutions or compromises before the larger group meetings. Mediation here is gathering information and then designing options for that information. The smaller group can choose options that they think will be agreeable to all parties.

What should designers do if this critical leadership role is lacking? In the first instance, it means the designer needs to fill in. The designer needs to come up with ideas and approaches that can bolster the work of the director or the producer. Not all directors have a strong visual sense. The designer needs to find ways to play to the strengths of the director. If the director is strong in language or psychological interpretation or ensemble building, for example, the good designer will find ways to use those areas as entry points into design discussions. The designer must learn the language of the director, at least in the early stages. It is also useful for the designer to watch the process of the director. Attend rehearsals. Talk with the actors. All sources of information in the early stages of a design are valuable. They may not all be used, but they are all valuable.

Listening is an acquired skill. It is an active, not a passive, process. It does not happen automatically for most of us. Designers are often eager to present their ideas. They are eager to jump in and make presentations, to jump to conclusions and begin building, to meet deadlines. But, as the lighting designer Pat Collins says, designing is "not about what the director says, but what the director wants."[1] This implies a more careful listening process—listening beyond the words to the needs or the vision that have not yet been articulated or communicated, a communication the designer can ar-

---

[1] Pat Collins, "Re: Interview," Telephone conversation with the designer, 10, May, 2001.

ticulate differently from the way a director might communicate it.

Early collaborative meetings between producers and designers or directors and designers should involve free-ranging discussions and impressions. This should be a period for uncensored conversation and multiple takes on the script or the project. This is a time for introducing open-ended questions rather than close-ended questions. Close-ended questions elicit a yes or no response. They leave little room for elaboration or detail. Open-ended questions allow for more possibilities. "Are you going to make the house red?" is a close-ended question. The answer is either yes or no. The answer leaves no room for a lead-in to other ideas. "What colors are you thinking about for the house?" is open-ended. This suggests a range of responses and maybe some more ideas about those choices. Close-ended: "Are the lights all white?" Open-ended: "What kind of palette are you thinking about for the lights?" Close-ended: "Are all the skirts going to be this color?" Open-ended: "What ideas were you thinking about in keeping the skirts in the same color range?" These are subtle distinctions but the collective impact is useful. Good designers need to come to these sessions fully prepared. They need to have researched the material, the period, the intent, and the goal.

The role of research in this process cannot be overemphasized. This is the beginning of preparation. Good designers need to fully immerse themselves in the dramaturgical history and time period of the project. This means learning to be an alien. Everything is new. You've just landed and everything is unfamiliar. No area of information is minor or inconsequential. Designers need to come armed with a range of ideas, not just one idea. Strategic shifts in approach can answer a range of questions: Does it offer a new view of the script? Does it change how we think about the subject or the author? Does it offer new perspectives on the themes? The creative growth that can develop out of these carefully gathered conversations is critical to the success of the venture.

Because the medium is visual, designers should augment their ideas and discussions with examples and sketches. Bringing in swatches, images, photographs, clippings, and art books as well as sketches can begin to move the conversations to a concrete and more specific level. Some designers will bring collage or *bricolage* (less formal collage with found objects and surfaces) presentations to these early discussions as a way of prompting consideration for the total effect of the production. A collage can coherently suggest the designer's current thinking about the design elements and their prioritized relationship to the project. The generalized nature of collage can also allow the other designers on the project to translate the collage ideas into their own design areas. As the director-designer Ping Chong notes, "Very early in the first decade of my work I was using the term *bricolage* because I was recycling material. I think of bricolage as taking something and recombining it in a new configuration. By recycling materials I was creating something new."[2]

All these materials should also be carefully gathered and reflect the specific thinking the designer is going through. It should not be a random and haphazard display of miscellaneous ideas, a kind of shotgun approach where the designer throws out too many ideas that are not carefully thought through in the hopes one will hit the producer or director's target. That can only lead to confusion or overkill. It should be as carefully gathered as the conversation that it prompts.

It is important to be flexible. Designers will often hit on an idea and enter the collaborative process with a kind of *idée fixe*—that is, "This is the best idea ever and let's not try to change it." A first idea or a first response to the text or project may produce some sense of comfort and security, but the practiced designer is open to other ideas and other approaches in an effort to find the best collective response.

A central strategy in good design is the use of metaphor. Metaphorical responses are a key to cross-communication in collaboration. Different people with differ ways of thinking and different ways of talking can sit at the same table by subscribing to a kind of *lingua franca*, a common language of understanding. By saying, "This play is like . . ." the effective designer is offering verbal bridges to visual concepts. Metaphorical design choices are organized around an accepted and useful figure of speech, where an object or description substitutes for the theme or main ideas of the project. Remember the discussion from the Introduction? We discussed a hypothetical production of *West Side Story* and began by comparing the musical to shards of glass. The metaphor served as an organizing device and allowed for specific responses from a variety of design areas that then maintained a coherence and unity.

---

[2] Ping Chong, "Re: Interview," Conversation with the director and designer, 22, September, 2003.

All collaborative discussions begin with limitless possibilities and resources. All collaborative discussions are tempered, soon, by limited possibilities and resources. Some ideas and strategies will be discounted simply because they are undoable. The production lacks the budget, the personnel, or the time. This is a time to consider the potential for those ideas under other approaches. The good designer will often find options here that meet the first expectation but that can come in under budget and on time.

We can borrow some strategies from conflict resolution professionals in an effort to improve collaborative discussions. It is often useful to identify others' ideas and presentations, not with a dismissive "I don't like that" or "I don't understand"; rather, it is more useful to begin with "What I see you suggesting . . ." or "What I hear you recommending is . . ." or "Tell me what you mean by . . ." The act of the question is a helpful way to continue discussion. If you are confused, ask a question. Jumping to a defensive posture of "I don't understand so it must be bad" helps no one. Questioning helps avoid breakdowns in communication and the shutting down of individual participants. And remember that questions are not critiques. If someone asks a question it may be for clarification. Don't take it as implied criticism.

It is important, always, to let the script or the project be the central arbiter of differences of opinion. This cannot be stated too often. Collaboration is about people working together. Sometimes that will mean a difference of opinion. Those differences cannot be merely power plays of one person's authority over another. If that happens, the point of the project can get lost. That can't help the production. Rather, the script is the policeman, if you will. It can break up the battles. Use the script to mediate through these differences of opinion. What evidence is there in the script or project to support your position? We must always return to the work at hand, the project, the script. This is the one common language, the touchstone we share in the collaborative process.

Finally, remember that there is a craft to collaboration, just as there is to conversation. Collaboration is a process one works at and acquires skill in. In terms of success, a certain percentage of each collaborative experience will be the personalities involved—what the individuals bring to the table in terms of their skills and interests. A certain percentage of each collaboration, as a process, will be the subscription to goals and objectives. A certain percentage of each collaboration will be the culture and history the participants bring to the table. If a particular collaborative experience was unsuccessful, it might be useful to go back and review what happened. What could have been done differently? If a production was particularly successful, such a review is equally useful and infinitely more pleasant. How can the experience be repeated? Learning how to talk, as designers, is one way of allowing our work to talk.

Designing for the Media

It is important to remember some distinctions between theatre and electronic media. The similarities between the two (narrative line, actors, directors, designers, dramatic action, and so on) can be helpful but they can also be deceptive. Theatre began as a verbal medium. It began with the word. The mythology of the theatre offers that the sixth-century Greek chorus was the nascent progenitor of Western theatrical tradition. When one of the chorus members (Thespis, it is said) stepped out from this chorus and spoke back to the group, dialogue was created.

The use of dialogue is central to the communication process of the theatre. This is why the playwright remains primary in the production process of theatre. As stated before, our search is for the intent of the playwright. Designers, directors, actors—all are engaged in an act of consensus building around what the play means and the source of that discovery process is the written page.

Electronic and digital media (including television, film, computers) are based in photography, the image. These media use the strategies of theatre (including words) but their genesis is the photographic image. Screenplays are about the description of events through visual images. The dialogue, the written word, generates the narrative, the arc of action in the theatre. The narrative, the arc of action in filmmaking, is generated by the images the camera records. Film uses dialogue, but the camera controls the information we see. Theatre cannot control, as successfully, all we (as the audience) see. The use of narrative in television for dramatic production (which can include situation comedies, made for television movies, and weekly dramas) is similar to that of film. The use of visual language in computer work (games, programs, the web) is dominant. In the electronic media we are visually composing for the screen (either the big communal screen in movie houses, the television screen in our homes, or the computer screen at our desks). The old argument, "Which came first, the picture or the word?" takes on significance when we determine how the medium is using tools to communicate with us.

Video games have introduced a kind of virtual theatre to the electronic mix. By allowing the game player (a virtual actor) to make certain decisions, to experience certain emotions, to interact with the narrative, the video game process introduces a new level of symbiosis, an integration of the actor and audience. The actual experience can be deceptive, however, because the game designers largely control the degree and limits of interaction, though the scripted range of possibilities increases exponentially with the memory capacities.

These media consciously or unconsciously take into account that we see images faster than we can talk. This is a singular difference with theatre. The origins of this ability to see images faster than we talk seem to be Darwinian; they are grounded in the survival skills of alert observation and timely reaction. This image-word dichotomy can result in major differences between media. The theatre is timed by the rhythm and speaking skill of the actor. Film and video can be timed by editing the image. Quick edits and flash sequences are possible in film, television, and video because of our ability to register those images more quickly than words spoken. This editing can further result in quick shifts of locale and dissolves or flashbacks.

These techniques can inform the process of screenwriting in distinctly different ways from those of a playwright. (There have been several significant attempts to meld the process of these two media distinctions. *Death of a Salesman* by Arthur Miller is often cited as an early engagement with filmic technique for theatre with mercurial shifts of locale, flashbacks, and dialogue that move in and out of disjunctions in time.) Designers, in turn, can respond differently to these hierarchies of word and image. (The set designer Jo Mielziner did so, again in *Death of a Salesman*. By using fragmentary set pieces and relying on lighting design for quick scene shifts and locale definitions, he was able to approximate the time shifts of film editing. The filmic technique of the dissolve was effected on stage by the use of scrim layers.)

We can further segment the work of designers into tangential areas such as event planning, parades, industrials, websites, and community-living design, among others. These are a few examples of activities that use the skills of design and designers in their realization. The great distinction that separates these ancillary categories is: Do they happen in real time (a temporal process) with a live audience? Theatre (real time, live audience) embraces the similar work of event planning (the opening of a mall or store, a parade, or an industrial presenting the newest model of a car). The photographic heritage embraces the electronic media's suspension of real time (quick edits and sequence images) even in ancillary activities (game shows, weathercasts, website design). Good designers need to begin their work by recognizing the differences between these two forms.

Film and Television and Digital Design

The theatre was one of the earliest venues for collaborative design. Using the skills of the architect, the painter, and the sculptor, design for the theatre quickly integrated into the service of expressing the intent of the playwright. This is a long history with several stylistic permutations. Good playwrights began to see the value of design and often would suggest specific choices as a part of the script and as a way of communicating intent. Film arrived much later. It is similar to theatre in narrative form but significantly different in presentation. There is a subtle shift from the ritualized nature of the live event to the mechanical reproduction of the elements similar to theatre such as acting, directing, set design, sound design, costume design, and lighting.

Film work, however, has developed its own visual and constructive language. Following on the technology of film is television, similar in many ways and more informal and personal in others. From these design forms we leap to the newest forms, design for video and computer work and design for the Internet. Website design is the newest field to integrate design elements into a system of recognizable intent. Each of these media creates certain expectations, challenges, and technologies. Think of the design process as a "cross-media" process.

Video Games

Designing for computer games is a vast field. It involves a whole range of individual artists, programmers, directors, managers, and technicians. The exponential nature of the software used in this field has led to extraordinary shifts in detail, focus, and range of design. Video game production involves roles similar to film and television production. There are producers who handle specifications and schedules and make the decisions on cost and keep to the time frame for production and introduction. Individual designers will often report to these producers. There is a specific category of designer who designs the game, usually from a game play point of view. Known as level designers, these designers take a game play description and create the environment in which the game is played. They are responsible for such details as architecture, texture placement, and character development.

These designers also have input into the graphic design of the game, though there is usually another category of designer working here. As with film and television there is usually an art director who has a larger managerial role and artistic oversight. The art director is usually a senior artist and may contribute substantially to the conceptual work of the game planning as well as individual assignments for various parts of the game. Individual digital artists will handle the model creation, texturing, and surface lighting.

Video game designers seem to be one in their admonition: "Don't let the technology seduce you. First ask, what do you want to do? Why? Then find the technology." They are suggesting that the technology cannot drive the design. The technology must facilitate the design. The same is true in the current design work for website designs. These media use the technology in a very conscious way. There is a "newness" to the methods that seems to become its purpose. The use of technology in service to the author's intent is still a promise, not a realization.

The prescient among us might argue that the next stage of development will be the virtual actor and the virtual locale. This is already the case to some extent with video games and some music videos. The technology is developing at a rate that allows the sampling of the real and the imagined in creative new combinations. We see virtual actors performing in a virtual set, both creations of computer-generated programs. The exponential relationship of the technology clearly points to the time when we will see virtual films or made-for-TV movies that have cast long-dead actors (digitally resuscitated) in new roles and in new spaces, all created by a computer.

When the level of realism in these situations reaches a point where the audience cannot detect the difference between the actual recorded space or actor and the computer generated one, then the new challenge will be what to do with this virtual actor and this virtual space? To look real is not enough. There is a difference between looking real and being believable. The touchstone is verisimilitude, or truthfulness to life. Does it seem real to the viewer? The spark of originality will come with the "soul," the difficult but critical introduction of human and spatial variables that render the image and locale believable. This is the work of designers and directors. If writers can continue to create new narratives, then the new directors and designers of this virtual world will lend credence and verisimilitude to the creations.

Event Design

Another area of design is event design. This type of design has its antecedents in such public celebrations as the *masques* of Inigo Jones, the garden entertainments of the French court, the morality pageants of medieval Europe, and the *carnaval* celebrations of the Caribbean and South America. Event design may or may not have a coherent narrative line. The "script" for the event could be loosely drawn from the participants or elaborated on with a more specific intent than just distraction. Event design can include the commercial work of industrials (product presentation for specific audiences, usually in theatricalized venues), parades, museum exhibits, and architectural detailing for planned communities.

The nature of these events shifts the relationship of the audience to the event. For parade and museum work, there is the presumption of movement on the part of the audience. The audience members may be shifting their perspective on the work by shifting their physical position. The audience member will also determine the time of the interaction; she may choose to stay in attendance or move on to other stimuli. Parades are sequenced units of time and stimulation. They may cohere in obvious ways (commercial interests, promotion, holidays, and so on) or less obvious ways (as in the Disney parades, which often invoke the collective memory of old animated films).

Theatricalized events use the strategies and design tools of theatre making to heighten the impact of the commercial nature of the offerings or to bring the varied stimuli of theatrical design to the sometimes less stimulating presentation of information or facts. Focus, intensity of presentation, traffic patterns (blocking in theatre), color, and balance can all alter the methods of presentation.

Website Design

Imagine for a moment a cube. The cube has six sides: a top, a bottom, a front, a back, and two sides. Then imagine that you can write on only one side. This seems to be the state of web design. There is a sense of horizontal orientation and vertical orientation. But the cube has volume. Put another way: imagine a proscenium theatre. There is a large curtain separating the audience from the stage. If as a designer you were restricted to writing just on the curtain surface to designate location and mood, you would be seriously restricted. But let the curtain rise and you suddenly have volumetric space. You have depth and an active cubic space in which to inscribe ideas visually. Good web design should use this idea of volume in designing the presentation of ideas and information. Unlike the stage, the use of an active diagonal (for example, moving from downstage right, floor level, to upstage left ten feet off the ground) is a practical possibility; it can be imagined on the computer screen and an illusion created.

Much of website design so far is on one plane. It employs the horizontal and the vertical. If there is animation, it is usually along those same planes. Much of website design is simple color blocks. Little attention is paid to texture. Note also that shapes and forms, as in theatre design, can take on values. The idea of round "buttons" for navigation is very different in feeling and response from rectangular ones. There has been a lot of attention paid to the navigational structure of website design. Some of this is similar to architectural navigation—how to lead people to a certain spot, efficiently, leisurely, or playfully. This is really a process of content management predicated on traffic patterns and intuitive logic.

But design can also play a role in this process. The logical or playful use of color, the sequences of textures, as well as depth movement and line movement, both real and by inference, can add dimension and interest when traveling the website. This can be extended to the idea of layering, perceiving objects in various planes receding to the background. Add sounds to this mix and the possibilities for shifts in attitude and response are greatly expanded. There is also the issue of screen size, the reference point. Even accounting for the various screen sizes currently available, we are still talking about mere inches of difference. The advent of wall screens may change these aspect ratios but for the moment the viewing area is quite constrained or, more positively, concentrated. There is a restricted amount of space for movement and expansiveness. Several websites still employ great stretches of white space to compensate for the concentration of visual assault that can happen with these small screen sizes.

The technologies, which will continue to evolve, impose gates, portals, or restrictions on the design process. Stated another way, the technology will continue to afford new opportunities for designers. For example, "web-safe palettes" allow colors to download successfully and quickly, responding to the range of equipment the viewer may have. As websites proliferate, the need for establishing individuality and uniqueness as attention-gaining strategies increases. Color still plays a dominant role in website design though movement is a close second. Texture has not been fully explored. Variety and contrast are underplayed and dimensionality remains two-dimensional. Virtual depth through object movement is just beginning to gain attention.

Websites are very personal. This is not a public interaction where one's presence is perceived as part of a collective. It is wholly individual. There is a privacy to the interaction with screen and viewer. We do not surf websites together.

Display Windows

For theatre designers, it can be instructive to study good window designs in department and specialty stores. There is an act of essentializing the message here, of selling an attitude (style) as well as a product. The window is a proscenium arch with backstage areas and onstage areas. The mannequin as actor becomes a template on which the viewers layer their own expectations. The designer will "costume" this mannequin and place the mannequin in a "set," the design of which is reduced to a single statement or use of elements.

This act of "visual reduction" helps to quickly grab the attention of the pedestrian, communicate the idea, and encourage entry. Good designers from all disciplines can learn from this strategy: How to most effectively and economically communicate the intent. The use of focused, directional lighting and the careful and disciplined selection of only those objects, set pieces, and props that contribute to the idea is a strategy that recognizes the visual power of selected images, especially in a culture of overstimulation. "Less is more" has never been more useful than in design. The Tiffany Company display windows in New York will often invoke nature with their first spring windows—for example, a simple (and expensive) diamond among the freshly sprouted blades of manicured grass.

This reduction of image is similar to the famous Andrei Serban production of *The Cherry Orchard*, where the placement of the characters in selected furniture pieces upon a vast white-carpeted ground cloth as the orchard invokes the essence of the Chekhovian ennui. The inside of the house became the outside orchard, snowbound. The visual metaphor quickly telegraphed the vulnerability of the characters and heightened our sense of their denial of events and reality, both financial and political.

Department store merchandising was an early example of taking design elements and manipulating them to a purpose, in this case to sell a product. The tools and techniques of theatrical design were appropriated for another kind of intent. The same appropriation has happened in the design areas most closely related to theatre: film and television. The skills of manipulation and opportunity afforded by these media have further been used in the ancillary fields of computer graphics and website design.

6
Case Studies

Flavius: Speak, what trade art thou?

from Julius Caesar
by William Shakespeare, Act One, Scene One

The following case studies should help the reader locate the possibilities for design in both an artistic and commercial setting. These individual profiles represent a sampling in the range of possibilities. Careful readers will observe certain common themes in these profiles. There is always the issue of collaboration. Inevitably each designer cites the need for collaboration as one means of avoiding isolation and expanding the range of possible choices in design decisions.

Equally, individual profiles highlight the need for intellectual and artistic nourishment. Many of these designers operate under strict deadlines. They need to produce and elaborate on design concepts with speed and intelligence. Many of these designers cite the need for maintaining a personal referencing inventory. This usually means going to museums, reading mythology, maintaining exposure to the visual and performing arts, and expanding the range of references in cultural terms such as history, psychology, sociology, archeology, architecture. This is an ongoing practice. It does not stop. It requires a degree of intellectual curiosity, an eagerness to know about new ideas, other ways of seeing, and historical experiments in medium manipulation. Many of the persons represented in these case studies have admitted to educating themselves in an ongoing way, not for edification per se, but as a way of building up an inventory of references and ideas that can be called upon when the need presents itself, especially in times of stress or deadlines.

In practical terms this means that the designer is always going to sources of inspiration and education. What do other cultures have in common with our own? How do other cultures define the issues I am dealing with? How do they manipulate the design elements? How have painters in the past used light to suggest emotion? How do sculptors use mass and movement to suggest intellectual themes?

How does this movie use the design element of color to visually code the different character relationships? How does this play's set design use line to foreshadow the demise of the lead character? How does the sound montage in this museum exhibit suggest the relationship between the village and the environment? These are all questions that the curious designer will ask on a conscious level. We will all be influenced by these design choices, but the active designer will mark these choices and add them to his own inventory of possibilities. These become a survival pack for future design choices.

Secondly, most of these designers admit to the importance of research as one way of jump-starting the ideas for a project. These are not research projects as in a classroom assignment. They are survival skills. Research, the immersion in the possible directions a design project may take, will offer up new choices and unexpected combinations. Such research is like the investment in a good brush to the painter. It will make for a better painting. Most designers develop a range of research options. There are visual libraries, the Internet, museums, print archives, motion picture archives, magazine collections, art books, reference libraries, museum catalogs, and art reproductions to name a few. Many designers will find personal favorites that dislodge visual blocks or help them move beyond the dreaded blank page. All designers have developed a library of useful materials.

This section explores a range of design options. Some of these areas represent a history of design engagement that is several thousand years old. Others are less than a hundred years old. Others are only a few years old. They each share the same basic manipulation of design elements though the medium through which they express themselves can be very different. As you read what these designers have to say about their work, try again to find the common threads that bind them across the media. Look for what they say about the script and intent. Listen for how they talk about design elements and notice how similarly they invoke collaboration as a strategy.

Each Character Has a Closet

Alyson Hui
Associate Costume Designer
The Guiding Light, Television

The Guiding Light *is the longest running soap opera on television. It began as a radio drama in 1937 and then made a successful transition to television. It has been broadcasting for over sixty-two years. Proctor and Gamble and CBS produce the show. The costume designer for* The Guiding Light *is Richard Shawn Dudley, and the costumes have been nominated for several Emmy Awards. Hui began her career by studying theatre design.*

"There is a big difference in designing for the theatre and designing for television and film. In the theatre everyone is going through the process together, at the same time and usually at the same pace. And the picture, visually, is much bigger in the theatre; you have to be much bolder. This means that there is a level of detail in film and television that is not there in the theatre. I know an actor who wanted a toe ring for a stage production. There is no way that a toe ring will be seen from the audience.

"Theatre is often about discovering layers of the character. Some of this comes from discussion sessions early on. This is not always the same in television and film. The designer may be exploring those layers on her own but the process is very personal and often on the fly. You don't have the same kind of time. Sometimes, when you do it right, it is very satisfying."

Hui notes that when designing for soaps, the designer is working with characters one already knows.

"This is an ongoing story. Each character has a closet, literally, where the clothing for that character is stored. This process is the same for episodics, running series, usually on nighttime, prime time, television. This existing wardrobe for this particular character can be augmented or changed with a new top or new coat. They can't wear the same thing every day or even every week, just as we don't. You have to plan it out, mix and match it. But the characters may be found in new situations or circumstances and then we have to design something new for them. And this process is usually very quick.

"Another issue in costume design for soaps is the look of the actor [the silhouette]. There are questions of weight and image. Does the actor look too fat or too thin? Does the producer think the actor looks too heavy? Sometimes it is the producer, sometimes the actor. There is a real tightrope to walk here. Sometimes an actor becomes pregnant. We've had five in the last five years! Then you need to determine whether that will be evident in the character. If not, how are we going to change the closet to hide the fact as much as we can? Sometimes actors gain weight and we have to adjust the costumes. Remember this is an ongoing process. We work with actors for years at a time.

"Designing for soaps is very demanding. You want to make it look real generally. But there are often fantasy elements written in that take the characters outside their current reality. There may be a Shakespeare-like moment, a dream sequence, or a fantasy. But we still have the characters we already know now placed in this new setting. We have two constraints. That's where it's fun. We once had a character who was a writer. So we had a chance to develop a whole set of costumes for the 1940s, as a fantasy segment for this writer's imagination. Since the writer was a longer-term character on the show, she was using this period often and we were able to develop an arc for the period. It was not just a one-shot deal. The characters were interacting with each other.

"Another time we had a character in a psychiatric ward and this was very rewarding. We got to do costumes for the inmates that were unique and different. I could distress, even, a button by cutting it in half. I gave a hat to one actor and said, 'You're always cold.' You get to be a little more creative. It's more than the everyday job of just getting the actors dressed—the 'What am I going to wear today' syndrome.

"You have to be careful of strobing in television."

Hui notes that this is where too many patterns are introduced and the camera animates these patterns because the lines are too close.

"There are also problems with colors, red and pink especially. You lose depth and tonality with these colors. If you do go with pink it has to be very, very pale. I know a producer for television who wants the costumes to be very bold, plain, large masses of solid color. This means little use of pattern or lines. The producer thinks people, when changing television channels, will be attracted to these bold solid colors and pause. The hope is they will become interested in the story because their eye has been attracted to the image. This can be a real challenge because you are really restricted. So you have to add in the details of, say, a purse or jewelry to add the depth and complexity. Lighting for television also restricts you, because the camera's ability to read detail in costume is limited and the lighting tends to wash out details like texture in the fabric.

"I get a script two weeks ahead. I'm working now on episodes that will air two weeks from now. As associate costume designer, I pull [the costumes for a character in] a particular show, an episode, from the existing closets for the characters and then the principal costume designer looks it over and we do a back-and-forth on the choice. Sometimes we disagree. What time of day is it? Where has the character just been? These questions help us arrive at the right choice. At that point we decide on the choice and that costume is set aside. When you're pulling the costume you also have to know what set they will be on. Will it be one of the ongoing sets for the soap or a new one? I need to know what colors the set has in order to pull the costumes. Either I will just go up and look at the set or talk with the set designer.

"I also need to know what gel color is being used [for the lighting]. Some gel colors will really change the fabric color and the way it is read by the cameras. You don't necessarily know what color is going to come out. This comes with experience, learning how colors read on the camera. This is also a problem with white. White usually has to be 'teched,' that is toned down, 'tea-d,' or softened with a brown or gray wash or tint [at one time literally with tea or coffee] because it reflects too much light. But there are always surprises. Everyone will be saying, in the control room, 'Look at that purple dress.' And you will say, 'What purple dress?' You realize the blue dress you brought for the character now reads as purple.

"On the day of the shoot, that costume is ready for the actor. They put it on and then go on camera. Usually there is no other process of approval, because no one has the time. This is for the day-to-day shooting. If it is a really big change, as with a flashback or fantasy sequence, or a period setting, then we will do sketches and go through producer approval. Then the process is just like theatre. We will swatch it then build it or rent it.

"Costuming sources for soaps are in three categories. The character's closet [the ongoing costumes] is the first. Another source is shopping a character. Here the costume designer actually goes out and 'racks' the costume, that is literally buys a garment off the rack of a department store without sketches or swatching. The final source is building [constructing] a new costume or renting a costume from outside sources [rental houses or theatre companies].

"Each soap has a different look. And the costume design choices reflect those different looks. Some soaps are very stark in contrasts of color. There is one soap that is very black on black, not very much color. These decisions really are the producers'. Unlike the theatre, the director has less choice because the director will direct only one episode. There may be five directors in one week. The consistency of the design is up to the producers.

"As the on-set designer, I have to be on call throughout the shoot. I stay in the control booth during the taping sessions in case there is a problem or changes are needed.

"Costume design for film work is more like theatre. You have a script. You break it down. You discuss choices. Your discussions are primarily with the director. Here you're talking concept. Occasionally the DP [the director of photography] will get into those discussions, and sometimes the actors. Sometimes these discussions can become tedious. You say, 'Do I really care where the mike boom is going to be?' The real difference between these forms and the soaps is time. You have to be ready on a moment's notice with the soaps. It's twenty times faster than the theatre."

Like Riding a Bike

Stephen Marsh
Production Designer, Hollywood

A production designer oversees all the visual design aspects of a film or television production. Stephen Marsh has worked in film and television in addition to his newest work in theme park design. His film work in-cludes George of the Jungle *and* Cool Runnings *for Walt Disney pro-ductions. He has also designed* Christmas Vacation, Big Top Pee-wee, *and* The Seventh Sign *among many other films. For television he de-signed the miniseries* A Woman of Independent Means, Lakota Woman: Siege at Wounded Knee, Truman, Purgatory, *and* Native Son, *among others. Marsh began his career working in the theatre.*

"Right now I'm working on a 3-D movie for a theme park ride in Osaka, Japan. These are called dark rides and this one is a 'pretend ride' because we really aren't going anywhere [unlike a roller coaster ride that travels actual distances]. This particular ride is just a theatre experience for little kids. It's very interesting because it requires three times as much light [to film] and much lower contrast in the sets, the set colors, because of the 3-D cameras. The film is very short, somewhere round ten or twelve minutes. This means you get a new audience about every fifteen minutes. If you make the film too long, people won't wait for the ride.

"It's like doing a commercial in an odd way because you have to be very clear; the audience will be seeing it for a very small amount of time. It needs to be simple and direct. Silhouettes need to be simple and clean. It's harder because you have to tell the story in a limited time. The script is always changing, too. It's not very different from theatre or film or television. It's still built the same way. There needs to be a beginning and a middle and an end. For this ride there are two scripts. There is a preride script and then the [actual] ride script. The preshow script is to build anticipation.

"When I first read a script I have to ask myself, 'Is there a chemistry here? Do I feel the story? Do I feel I'm feeling it the way the writer felt?' The writer is the first spark. I'm very interested in what the writer has to say. So when I first read the script, perhaps oddly for a designer, I'm interested more in the character than I am in the locale. The mood and the characters create the story. After story, I read the script again for the locales, the sets that are needed. Then I try to tie that back to the characters. How do the characters live? What do they do? What kind of diners do they eat in? What kind of cars do they drive? I want to know what kind of people they are because I'm telling a story.

"I have to think about all the colors, the textures, the shapes of things and how they are going to contribute to the story, the arc of the story. When I read the script the second time, it's kind of like, oddly, riding a bike. Everything in life is like riding a bike. Because first of all when you get on the bike you are not interested in where you are going, you are interested only in mastering the skills to stay up. As you get better, better at the balance, it becomes second nature, and you become interested in where you are going. So I am not so interested in the process of design when I first read a script, that's the balancing part. I'm interested, rather, in where I'm going. I begin to get strong impressions about the chemistry of the script. With good writing I get strong impressions, things become specific, shapes and colors. How furniture should be. What kinds of pictures are on the walls.

"At other times, with bad writing, I don't get strong impressions, so I have to make it up or go talk with the writer and the director. In a perfect world I can go sit and talk with the director, the director of photography, and maybe the creative producers. Then we can get inside the character's head. Sometimes we don't have to do that. It's just there. It's on the page. Sometimes it's not. It may be more sparsely written. Maybe the writer is only interested in plot, not interested so much in character, then we have to start giving character and it becomes harder work . . . but still interesting work.

"We all become a camera when we read the script. We can't help it. Any book. Any novel. All of us. Every human being. We can't help becoming the camera. We see the people. We see the spaces they live in. We sense the volume. Does this person live in a small space? Do they live in a big house . . . or a bus? Sometimes the space will contribute to the arc. The character may start off very poor at the beginning of the picture and then [become] wealthy at the end. The character then may start off in very small spaces and end in very big spaces. Or maybe you go the other way around. You start off at the YMCA, a huge place, and the character is lost, and you end up in a cottage by the sea.

"They are expecting, as they say, for me to 'bring something to the party.' You can't go to a party empty-handed in Hollywood. You have to come in with a take. The trick of course is that you have the same take or something like the same take as the director or the producers. If you have a slightly different take, something that's more unique and yet it's within the scope of what they are thinking, then that's great. That's wonderful. Then they will think, well he's going off a bit on a tangent but we can adjust. If you have a completely different take, you probably aren't going to get the job.

"If the designer being interviewed thinks it should all take place in a concrete bunker but the script is set in a grand hotel in Nice, France, then what? You have to be somewhere close to what the writer wanted. If you have an original take on it, if you say, 'Wouldn't it be great if this was not just a hotel in Nice but it's the most modern hotel in Nice, not an old-fashioned, gilded one but a great modern one.' Maybe then the producers will think, 'Yeah, that's a great idea, maybe we should get away from the old idea of the grand hotel.' Then if you are hired, they are saying, 'This is the kind of thing we want. We are going to adjust it. But at least we are in the right ballpark.' Then it becomes meetings all the time, every day, sometimes many times a day.

"In working with a producer, I never say 'no.' I don't say, 'No, we can't do that.' I don't say, 'No, I don't like that idea.' Because you know, there are no bad ideas, really. Maybe they are different from mine, but it doesn't mean they're bad. I might have to go think about it. Maybe it is a better idea. And if it is a better idea, I need to know how to go with it. It can [also] be very important what the director is not saying. Sometimes directors can unwittingly be talking about one thing but it's something else going on in their head and you have to look through and see what it is. And turn the conversation around so that they find out what it is.

"We talk about the look constantly and the story points, how we're going to turn them. Sometimes very specific details: What kind of music would the character be listening to? What kind of shoes do they wear? What kind of floor do they have? What kind of faucets on the bath taps? Everything you see in the movie has been carefully worked out, especially in movies that have cost some money. Everything that's there should be telling the audience something. Everything there should be a clue. Take a wall switch. Is it just bare wires? Or a decorative wall plate? Or is it one of those clear plastic protective plates? That could tell you something about the character. They may not want us to get our dirty hands on their walls. Touching them. They think we are dirtier than they. That can tell us something about the character. Even if it's going on subconsciously, I want to make sure there are as many clues there for the audience as possible. It should be as full of the experience as we can get on the screen. It's not like the theatre where you have plenty of time to look at the set. We have sometimes only seconds for the set.

"In the same way, you may have noticed that people never walk up a full flight of stairs. They take the first three and the last five or the first five and the last three unless there's a story point. If it's just someone going upstairs to an apartment you're not going to waste time with walking up a whole flight of stairs. You want to get to the point of the movement. The audience, again, fills in the middle, the blanks. Something was implied and the audience believes they saw it.

"Then we have to think about how we are going to photograph this. Are we going to deep focus? Wide lenses? Or shoot it with long lenses, 'stack everything up' as the cinematographers say, making everything out of focus except the characters? Sometimes we need to isolate the characters, and so with long lenses we can throw the background out of focus and isolate the characters and the audience with them.

"It's important that I know how it's going to be shot because I have to design for that shot. What kind of lighting? Maybe we're going to light harshly, from the top, or maybe strip lights over a table, to give shadows to the face, to the eyes, to the scenery. Then I have to give a reason for how light would come in there. Maybe it's a skylight. Hard light coming into a dark room. It would depend on what kind of mood. Is it night? Is it day? And remember, we don't build anything that's not photographed. If the camera moves to the edge of a door that's where the set will end. I have to be exact and I have to be economical, because I have budgets to worry about, too.

"As a production designer I have to work very closely with the set decorator and as much as possible with the costume designer. The art director and set decorator and I meet every day and talk all the time. Their offices have to be close to mine. I want to talk to the costume designer, also, as much as possible. As early on as possible. Then I might say, 'You know, we're thinking about very flowery sets, and maybe the costumes should be in solid colors so they can jump out.' We don't want the costumes and the set making the characters disappear. We want to make sure we can see them. We need to have those discussions early on. We usually come to an agreement pretty early on, on palette. We'll limit the palette for the show. The palette may have an arc but we want to nail that down early. Then I have to find locations that will be inside the palette. After all, we can't be painting a whole town.

"We shot much of *Citizen Cohen* [HBO] in Pittsburgh. Pittsburgh has wonderful older buildings that look very governmental. We needed to get shots that appeared to be in Washington or New York a lot of the time. So we had a lot of standing scenery, if you like. This is where design becomes a process of choosing something, not just drawing something. Sometimes choosing the locations, the right locations, is very important to creating the mood. We couldn't build a lot, we didn't have a very big budget, so we had to choose carefully and not have to redress a lot of streets.

"On *Cool Runnings* my idea was to use the Jamaican flag colors and the brightness of those colors introduced to the white, the bleaker winter landscape of Canada. I talked with the costume person about the idea of bringing color with them and life and light. [They needed to bring] the colors from Jamaica. And we needed to see that in the hotel rooms, in the wallpaper, in what they're wearing.

"On *George of the Jungle* we looked at footage shot in a rain forest in Australia. I didn't like those [images]. They were dark and forbidding. When we first started this film, Disney said, 'Remember, this jungle has to be happy. We're making a live-action version of a cartoon show.' So we needed the jungle to be bright and happy. It shouldn't have dark corners and things hiding. We decided instead to shoot the wide exteriors in Hawaii and then build the jungle on a stage in Los Angeles. [They] had to match. We also had to change how we lit the leaves. [Often in film,] the leaves are all lit from the top; the leaves become white and hot spots. It looks strange. Leaves lit from the top don't look right. So we decided to light from the back. Light coming through the leaves. They light up much more and become greener and they become happier. There was also a clear decision on the choice of plants. Nothing with sharp leaves. We had to make sure it looked happy, and round, and warm.

"*Muppets in Space* posed different problems. If you are building a set in which both a Muppet and a live actor are to appear, then you have to build it to the scale of the actor. You can't have live actors walking in small doors. But you can sneak in shifts in scale. Maybe the Muppet is at a smaller desk. If you are shooting a scene in which just Muppets appear, you can go down to the Muppet scale. But this scale is a weird thing. It is not a continuous scale. It depends on what character is in the scene. If it's someone like Kermit the Frog you can build the set to Kermit's scale. I had some say in the colors, but that was restricted. Not much on the Muppet colors or costumes, those were already set, but I could say if something was going to be too bright. For film, of course, red can 'sing' too much, especially if you do a video transfer for later showing. I had to design sets that kept the Muppets in the foreground. You can't put them too much in the background or in the middle ground and you need to put them behind things. Because Muppets don't have any feet. Mostly Muppets are in close-up in the foreground so you don't go too deep with the sets.

"I did a miniseries for television, *A Woman of Independent Means*, that had 186 sets. I have a research book on that film that is about 2½ inches thick. I do a lot of my own research and I send the production assistants out also to do research. They go out to the library or more online now and download all kinds of things. But we still have to get on the phone and talk with people. I remember talking with a chap who was a specialist with telephones. You can get on the web anything you need about what a 1952 phone looked like.

But I wanted to know the process of making a call. Which way was it? Did you wait for a dial tone and then put in a dime or did you put in the money and then get a dial tone? This became important for the actors, for the action. And I knew when the phone was on the set, the director was going to ask, 'How do you use this thing?' I had better know. I can't say, 'I don't know.'

"In *Lakota Woman* there was a flashback to 1890. The American Cavalry was supposed to be jumping over some barbed wire in a field. I did a lot of research trying to find out what barbed wire looked like in 1890. It probably was important to no one else, but it was important to me. I want to get things right. I think I have a responsibility. I don't want people looking back at these films and saying oh, this is okay and it being wrong. After all film is also a historical record. If you're doing history and pretending that it's real . . . you better do it right.

"I don't like to do the same thing twice. I like to change mediums. I like to pop back and forth between film and television. Sometimes the really interesting projects are where you least expect them. There will be another shift as we move from film to digital videotape for movies. We watch film right now; in the future we will be watching a television picture in movie theatres. At present, digital video doesn't have the depth of color, the nice black shadows. Film has an enormous range and is deeper, more detailed. But the image will eventually go directly from a camera to a hard drive. With special effects, we now have to go from film to digital tape and then back again. This is a long and expensive process. With digital there are fewer steps and it is more economical. And it's faster.

"The shift from film to television currently is very different. With film there is a lot of depth, a lot of detail. Now film is only one plane, it is not actually dimensional. But there is the sense of a lot of depth. Television doesn't have much depth. And the screen is still pretty small. There are only a limited number of colors we can use for broadcast."

Marsh is referring to the standards the National Television System Committee set to make the transition from black-and-white television to color broadcast a compatible system. That system limits which colors can be used for broadcast and still maintain compatibility with black and white receivers.

"And the television screen uses many more close-ups. The key is to keep it simple, keep it clean. It shouldn't be too cluttered. The audience will accept cleanliness. It doesn't need to be a jellybean jar all the time. But with film it can be. You're looking at a much bigger, wider screen. You can look at the background. You can see all kinds of stuff going on. You have a much better chance to tell the story. There are a lot more pieces to the puzzle, a lot more detail. Television is more of a challenge. You have to tell the story with fewer props. And they have to be absolutely right. The background is usually thrown out of focus, and together with close-ups that gives you more depth. Good design is the removal of unnecessary detail. Don't have a toaster on the table if no one is making toast. You don't put things there, just to have things. That isn't part of design. Design is driven by plot, by character.

"Texture is more important, oddly, in black-and-white work. It needs to be lit right; it needs to be cross-lit to pick it up. Look at the early black-and-white movies. People look especially rugged. They are in open weaves and linens because texture was the other way of creating depth. But texture in theatre work has many more freedoms. They are not stuck to reality. Though film has, in the last few years, been a little freer, especially with all the fantasy movies being made.

"Earlier in my career I was more uptight about things like texture and palette. I did *Native Son* and it was again like balancing on the bike. If I did it again I wouldn't be worrying about it, it would just happen. But in *Native Son* I was trying to tie together several locations. Some were in Chicago; some were in downtown Los Angeles. We were all over the place. So trying to tie together all these rooms to look like one courtroom and jailhouse, I used dark woodwork as the emblem; that took us all the way down to the bottom of the stairs and then at the bottom, at the jail, all the colors went to gray. And became aged. It had to be like a descent into hell.

"In the film business, there is time between pictures. I think having time to paint and read biographies and history a bit helps. All those feed. I get an awful lot by watching other movies. I don't pay much attention to design; I get involved in the plot. Unless I'm looking at the design to vote [for the Academy Awards]. The best designs shouldn't be too much there. They should be there to back up the actor.

"Keep your ideas simple and big. Because if you have others nibbling away at them, the ideas can stay intact. And don't worry about your design ideas getting watered down. It will probably help in the long run. Most of what you will be trying to do is create things that tell us stories. Try to enjoy it. And always collaborate. Try to find a way to make your ideas heard, certainly, but do look at other people's ideas as well. Anything that can help you. The cinematographer may have a great idea for a bedspread."

The Last Cold Eye

Pat Collins
Lighting Designer, Broadway

Pat Collins has worked extensively as a lighting designer for theatre (both Broadway and regionally), opera, and dance in the United States and Europe. Her Broadway credits include, among others, Ain't Misbehavin', Three Penny Opera (for which she received a Tony nomination), I'm Not Rappaport (for which she received a Tony award), Sherlock's Last Case, Conversations with My Father, The Heidi Chronicles, The Sisters Rosensweig, Once upon a Mattress (1996), A Delicate Balance, A Moon for the Misbegotten, and Proof. In opera, she has designed for the Metropolitan Opera, Washington, San Francisco, Los Angeles, and Houston grand operas. She has designed throughout Europe including stints with the English National Opera, Opera North, Scottish Opera, the Glyndebourne Festival and the Royal Opera House, Covent Garden.

"My interests in lighting design began with a fine extracurricular theatre program at Brown University. There was no theatre department at that time and I was a premed student anyway. But when I decided to do theatre, I *really* wanted to do theatre so I looked around and found a great Spanish literature professor, a Cervantes scholar. I studied with him while I was doing extracurricular theatre. The theatre work was very disciplined, very focused. I went through all the technical departments one could go through. When I got to lighting I knew that was where I wanted to be.

"Technical preparation is nothing. Anybody can learn that. In terms of design, the technology is just a tool. Very simple stuff. The key for me was a liberal arts education. A renaissance attitude toward information.

"That kind of education gives you a larger tapestry to view. You can work out your own patterns. Because design, ultimately, is only about the quality of the human being. It's not about a school. A school can give you technical information. It's about the designer, the creator. How you use the technology is who you are.

"I don't think about technology when I read a script. I think about form, texture, color. I think about tempo. I think about essentially the same things a good painter would think about. Technology is just the brush. A painter, again, will pick a certain kind of brush to do a particular thing. You will use aspects of the technology to allow you to do that thing—a difference in the texture, a difference in the tempo, a difference in the attack. You have to construct some form in response to how you're feeling about the thing you're doing. You use the tools at hand.

"A lot comes out when you are doing the collaborative part. You go with your emotional response to the material. You learn to look deeply into what your co-artists have done with the director. A set designer and the director work together; they are essentially the structure of the piece. Look at what that is. Never mind what they say it is. Look at what in fact they are doing. You try to uncover it.

"There is often a very passionate relationship between the set designer and the director. They battle out their positions in what is the world of the piece. They come usually to a mutually shared attitude about what the piece is. We [lighting designers] don't have to have long conferences, it's right there. A costume designer, on the other hand, must get more into the research of the period of the piece.

"It's about time. Time and place. Sometimes the director will have strong ideas about what the piece is to look like. The set and costume designers share a much more intimate relationship with the director and the material than the lighting designer does. Almost all of the intent of the piece is finished by the time the lighting designer looks at it. Whatever those battles were, whatever the director felt, is going to show up. I am there to deal with what they have done. My job is revealing what they have done. I think of the lighting designer as the last cold eye. I am really not interested in long conferences with a director about what they think they are going to do. Because invariably what they think they are going to do is not what they end up doing. I have not been listening to the long discussions about what the piece should be. I'm looking at what is there. No amount of conversation makes the work clearer than what's onstage.

"Lighting doesn't change anything. Lighting is revelation. It's a form that reveals. It doesn't override. It can be bad but ultimately it is light falling on objects on a stage. That's it. What the objects are is what you will see. The organization of the light should reveal what is there. It is not to itself alone. I serve the piece. I serve the director. And by extension I serve the other designers. I am not the party of the first part. I am not the primary initiator. If I have a concept outside that which the director and other designers have done, it is inappropriate.

"The script will give you a feeling for the form. Then you have to find a way to express that form. What will the piece become when it gets on its feet from the first rehearsal, when the director and actors start working? This will give you the most revealing glance into what the work will be. I look at shape in these rehearsals. I look at emotional content. Depending on how naturalistic the script is, I look for the clues. What time of day is it? Where is the scene taking place? What is really going on?

"About color in lighting—you can push color, but that usually depends on the set designer and the costume designer. If a costume designer has put an acid green onstage, then I'd better not turn it to mud. The designer has made this color choice for a very specific reason. I may punch it up but I must not weaken it. If you understand that light is intended to reveal, then you understand what a lighting designer's final job is. It is not to make another statement; it is to uncover what is there.

"Collaboration is not about talking. It's about the script. It's about revealing to one another what each sees in the text. When you get in there, in the trenches, trying to function as a designer, it's how you think, how things are revealed to you, what you see.

"I have been doing lighting design a long time. There is nothing about it that surprises me. Nothing intimidates me. But I see the text in a way the director doesn't. The director may be saying something to me about the lighting, but I am not listening to the specifics of that information, I am looking for what the director has in mind. What is behind those statements?

"This is a musical form really. If transitions are not there, if the attack is not there, there is little I can do to change it. Lighting, like music, is movement in time.

"The lighting designer is there, at all the rehearsals. Usually the costume and set designers are not. When I do a Broadway show, I can be in rehearsals for weeks. I just finished a show at Lincoln Center. I was there for four weeks, and that was after previews had begun. I know a lot about the piece by the time I design it.

"Lighting designers are collectors. Designers are visual collectors. In our brains we make pictures. In our brains we think in pictures. The questions we ask are almost always about what we see. The things that cause us problems are almost always about what we see. For me, the organization of that information, how we deal with it, why we deal with it, is intimately attached to what I see: the images.

"Good designers as well as good directors are not always about giving answers; they are about asking questions. Curiosity is the key; curiosity about movement, about texture, about tempo. Can something be made ugly? Can something be made beautiful? Everything you create relates to that which pleases you. And what pleases you comes from who you are.

"I think that probably at this stage of the game, I am almost more of a dramaturg than I am a lighting designer. Dramaturgy is like a detective game. I find that exciting. How small things fit one into another. It's like a puzzle. It probably begins instinctively with the writer. You put things together and you see how the pearls are strung out.

"We can only teach technique. We cannot teach design; that is in the eye of the person, in the spirit of the person. You can teach a technique and hope that it will serve. You cannot say it is the only way. You can say: this is a tool; it may be right for you, it may not be right for you. This is what I can show you. It is, again, like a brush.

"You have to confront yourself. This is, ultimately, what design is about. What you are is what you put into your design."

A Treasure Hunt

Alison King
Web Producer, Website Designer
San Francisco

Website design represents one of the newest forms of design and media. While the medium itself, digital in form, is evolving with the technology, some of the strategies for collaboration and the role of design in that communication resonate with other design areas.

"My last project was for a branch of Sony Music. There was a development office with a portfolio of companies and my job was producing any site that those companies needed. It was a wide range of projects because every company was different. My job was to work with the people at these companies and the people at Sony to create different sites. Sometimes this involved making a company website.

"The work involved scripting. The script is really the user experience: what the user sees and in what order; the experience they have sequentially when they come to the site. What do we want them to see first? What is the most important thing on the 'page'? How do they know quickly and easily what the site is about and where they can go? This is navigation, site organization. Should it be a linear experience, an actual script for the user where they walk through a site in a certain way? Or should all the information be laid out and [we now let] the user determine where to go, what happens? On more complicated sites, we get into the issue of 'user experience.'

"Sometimes you work extremely closely with a client. The logo and the color schemes. The basic visual images. A large part of my job is learning how to work with people, collaboration. I need to learn to speak the language of all the different kinds of people who are working on the site. If you are speaking to the marketing department and they are using a certain language, the HTML [HyperText Markup Language, a nonproprietary method of coding text] engineers who are actually building the site may not understand. My job is to go between the departments and make everybody understand. To explain why a page can't behave in a certain way, why it's technically not going to work. I have to make sure everyone understands the limitations, where we are in the process. I have to facilitate an understanding.

"With large companies, in creating websites there will be a design department, an engineering department, and a marketing or development department. For example, my first job was with *PCWorld*, making their magazine a website with content changes each month. That was very big. One department would sell ads on the site. Another department would plan editorial direction. Some [engineers] were even designing a search engine for the site. There was software that could be downloaded.

"If you're just a web shop, a small company developing websites, then the number of people working will be smaller. Several people will have several jobs. As a producer I had learned a little bit of everything and had not specialized. I did design for a while. I did programming for a while. I have a [background] also in journalism that helped me communicate with editorial departments.

"When I'm designing there is often not a lot of freedom in design [element] choices. You are working with an [existing] logo and the company's colors. They want a certain design. You go into a meeting and everybody says 'green' so the site has to be green. The most difficult thing, if you are trained in more traditional art or painting, is that color on the screen works differently. It is [made] differently and functions differently. Light color combinations are [different] from [pigment] colors. Cyan and magenta are physically different. If you are working with a paint program and you are used to mixing [pigment] colors a certain way, that won't work [for the paint program]. The rules are different.

"The web is very influenced by itself. At any given moment designers will all start using a certain typeface. It catches on and all the sites are using it. Certain color combinations become really popular. Color schemes reflect trends. Right now there are more interesting muted colors [being used]. When I first started I was told bright green was the most attention-grabbing color and that if you were developing a site you should use bright green. You need to know what people's eyes are drawn to but there is also the influence of general trends. Color schemes get associated with certain websites and certain companies. The colors are more abstract; they are not object centered.

"My personal web style as a designer is always to be as simple and clear as possible. I like minimalists' designs. If you have a certain shape and you repeat it as a button [a navigational element], if it makes sense to people using the site, then you can reinforce that with maybe a button that then lights up a certain color and you know you're now on the right page. A combination of color and line will help make things easier on the user.

"But then it all depends on the client. The first thing you do when you sit down is say, 'Who is this for?' 'What is your user like?' If it's just you or your family then you have real freedom. If the user is someone who never uses the web except to make a purchase every few months then it may need to be more [guiding] and the design may need to be very simple.

"There is an accepted standard that there is a navigation bar on the left. There is a banner across the top and the most important things are in the middle, similar to print layout. It's recognizable and easy and sets up some kind of standard. You want people to get to the information as easily as possible. If they have to start from ground zero every time it can be confusing. You essentially have a [series] of screens and the user has to move through them.

"Animation can be really powerful. For a long time there wasn't much animation, then advertising used it. If your site has advertising you have to [balance] your movement with the advertisement's movement. Or at least consider it. The trend now is to use 'flash' on a site. This is a coding tool that allows the user to click on different parts of the animation and move to different areas. There will very often be a kind of flash intro now that gets the user's attention. All of the parts of the site, for instance, may swirl around the screen and then fall into place.

"I've seen texture used in really interesting ways on sites. Things can be blurred. Or you can take a photo and distort it [with texture]. But with the day-to-day, more informational sites, there's not a lot of texture being used. It depends on the site. If the site is a destination, a place where people have come to look, then those [elements] may play a larger role.

"My rule is always, 'Who is your user?' You try to figure out who your target audience is. You want them to be taken in by your site. You want them to be entertained, not annoyed. It's hard to generalize about the web because it's so varied. There are so many sites with [different] purposes. Some sites are just there to be cool, to look cool. The site designer doesn't care about you finding the content; they just want it to look good. But [that wouldn't work] for your city council website.

"My interests are in technology and design, and content. This is a whole new form of media. It's more like television and radio but the design is not as direct.

"I [like to] go to websites. I also like computer games and Japanese art. You have to really like the work. Browsing the web is the best way to get new ideas. There's so much out there. It's kind of a treasure hunt."

A Chair Becomes a Mountain

Ping Chong
Director, Designer, New York

An experimenting theatre artist, Ping Chong is referred to as a director, a choreographer, a video and installation artist, and a theatre designer. He is an OBIE award winner, a Guggenheim fellow, as well as the recipient of many foundation awards. He has created over thirty works for the stage since he began in 1972. Together with Meredith Monk he directed two television specials, one of which, Turtle Dreams, won the Grand Prize at the Toronto Video Festival. Chong created environmental pieces for the Visual Arts Center at the Massachusetts Institute of Technology *and was exhibited at the Venice Biennale, among others. At the time of this interview he was working on a new piece,* Blind Ness, *developed out of research into the Belgian king, Leopold II (1835–1909), whose brutalizing occupation of the Belgian Congo led to an estimated five to ten million deaths. The performance piece was scheduled to open in New York later that year.*

"Very early in the first decade of my work I was using the term *bricolage* because I was recycling material. I think of bricolage as taking something and recombining it in a new configuration. By re-cycling materials I was creating something new. I still draw a lot from existing sources, and then reconfigure. [Bricolage] is still there but I don't like to be tied down to a single concept. It becomes too narrow. I do use found sources these days, especially in terms of text, but the shows I do aren't just about text. There is sound. I was really [an early user] of sound in theatre. It was a natural thing for me. My very first show was as much about the perception of sound as it was about the perception of light. It was about sound and light and space, not about narrative. Narrative was something to hang the event on. I came out of film. I used recorded sound right from the start. It never occurred to me not to. I was very conscious of sound as a design element. I understood it as being primary.

"I started out in visual arts. And then I graduated in film. My family never encouraged me to be in the arts, [though] they were in the arts. My father, my father's brothers, my grandfather, my mother all were in the Chinese opera. My father's side of the family was all theatre. My mother was the first theatre person in her family. They didn't encourage or discourage me in the arts. They would say, 'You're going to starve to death.' But they didn't stop me from doing it. As a kid I was into dinosaurs and knights. By the sixth grade I was drawing cartoons, which were movies. I had my friends playing the parts. My whole thing was films. I would see thirty films in a summer. I'd go to two double features a day until I'd be kicked out. Movies were a very big part of my life.

"My early work was [also] very conscious of space. How to play with foreground, background. Maybe because I came out of film, I'm always operating in a frame. I'm an artist who likes working in a proscenium. I like controlling the image. On a thrust stage you can't control the image the way you can in a proscenium. I'm always about making pictures and combining different media. There [are] always projections. I think of the stage space less as a stage designer than as a visual arts project. It is forms in space—volume, color, and texture.

"The thing about a fluid space, like a dance space, is that it interests me [because of the fact] that my first theatregoing experiences were in the Chinese opera. There a chair can become a mountain. It's fluid. I don't like the rigidity of [realistic] Western theatre. A library set, for example, doesn't allow the space to be plastic. Theatre is about plasticity, of space, the use of space and time. Literalism is deadening. It has nothing to do with the imagination, nothing to do with the essence of theatre. Greek theatre wasn't like that.

"But we seem stuck in a kind of naturalism, maybe because we're such a materialistic society. Have the new technologies produced a new kind of theatre yet? There are isolated examples, but it's expensive. Theatre can't afford that. Stage spaces, though, should be transformative. I don't want a library [set] that's realistic and just sits there. I want radical designs for classical plays! Not being realistic frees you up. You can't compete with [realism] in film and television. But the theatre is human contact. Fundamental. Without machines. It's like the difference between taking a train or a plane and walking or riding a horse. The train and the plane change human time.

"My roots in performing arts are in dance. That becomes fundamental to the way I use space. Not build walls and sets, but a space [that] is more fluid because of my own dance background. There [needs to be] space for movement. Because I'm interested so much in all the arts, I drew so much from them; I really am more an interdisciplinary artist. My frame of reference is a lot of different things. It's not really theatre. I describe myself as a visual artist who happens to work in a live medium. I don't see myself as a theatre artist. My roots are visual arts and film. [They include] watching my parents as a child; watching [their work] in Chinese opera. Film is still my great love. [But] I have no interest in making films and I have no patience for a medium that's all tech. It takes a day to shoot two minutes. I don't have that patience. But still I know more about film and the other visual arts than I do about the [remaining] arts. I know dance by default. I came from that medium, even though I was ambivalent about it. I danced with Meredith Monk but I never trained that hard. It was a time when it was about natural movement. I was not a technical dancer. That was not my ultimate interest. My interest was always in being 'the maker.'

"[Yet] even though I'm a control freak I want people to contribute. I want to draw the best of their creativity out. I will usually throw an idea at them and then have them evolve it and bring back something of their own. I want the images to be memorable and if it's really not fitting my vision, I let people know. It's really about how accurately you communicate your needs and it's also about trusting the people you're working with and challenging their creativity. With my current project I said to the set designer, 'You know I want those kinds of floats or wagons that have a funky, homemade look, colorful, childlike.' And then he has to show me what he thinks it will look like and I have to say 'No, yes, no, yes.' For example, with the floats, there's a moment where a hut is seen to be burning and a native is on the floor with flames on his back. And the scene designer said, 'These figures are flat, right?' and I said 'No, they're not flat. They can't be flat. They have to be three-dimensional.' Those are important differences.

"And then I was thinking if there's a tray [needed] are we going to use some period tray with china? I thought, 'That's too boring.' Maybe we should just have a rectangular, minimalist black surface, stylized to match the black aspects of the set and costumes, not to be period about it. But that's still a thought. It's not set yet. It's about what works—pragmatic in a lot of ways. I decided on the float idea because they are freestanding. They all have wheels and they are all meant to be in this parade that happens about two-thirds into the show when the audience *knows* what the story is about. Then when the floats come through it's kind of like a summary of what we've been talking about. Then we can move to the end of the show. There is a convergence at the end. But the parade elements will be in the show earlier, but only as pieces. They serve as kind of sentinels; then when they are all together they are really telling the story in a visual way, as a parade. There will [also] be Bunraku puppeteers on stage."

Bunraku is a Japanese theatre form dating from the seventeenth century. Bunraku combines puppetry and narrative. Often several puppeteers (visible onstage) manipulate the puppets with complex, realistic movement and facial expression. Bunraku productions are accompanied by traditional Japanese musical instruments and often elaborate scenery.

"Maybe they will be in black . . . or maybe gray. It's tricky. We don't know yet. Because the show is in process we don't always know what props we'll need. That's why I'm trying to find a solution, one, that's interesting and, two, that's not always trying to be kind of literal about everything. We do need some amount of period, [but] I want the audience to be able to relate to this story. It is really a story of spin. [I want them to ask,] 'Why does this all sound so familiar?'

"My thing about collaboration is really about my need for engagement. It's not that I can't figure it out on my own if I really had to. But I don't have the time to do that. I've got enough on my plate. That's why they [the designers] are there. They're professionals and it's their job to do it. I've talked to the costume designer about how the costuming should be elegant, but because [actors] are playing multiple characters the beards or wigs have to come off really fast so they don't need to look as realistic. They can be about 'theatre.'

"My head is always about that control thing. I started out on this project thinking, 'Well, maybe I'm going to let the piece be messier,' but in the end it never winds up being messy. It winds up being very carefully thought out. This may be a personality thing. It could go back to living in a household with four other siblings in a very small immigrant [space] where the house was total chaos. Now my space is anything but chaotic. I need a kind of clarity around me. That translates into my work. That kind of precision is why I relate so much to Japanese aesthetics. In that sense I'm closer to the Japanese than I am to my own culture, which is Chinese. There is a sense of precision and clarity. And I'm a pragmatist. I understand the use of space. If you make one area very chaotic and the rest is very clean, the contrast makes things bigger.

"Managing the media in a production is like a three-ring circus. I have to trust the people I've chosen to work on my projects. I work with the same people as much as possible. I rarely work with a designer *once*. If I work with a designer once, then there's a reason for that. On this project my set designer is also my lighting designer, which I love. Because he's lighting the set and the two need to talk to each other and they are the same person. All the designers need to sit down and talk to each other. They need to be clear about whose job is what. For example, the show needs puppets and scenery. And the set designer asked, 'Are the puppet element in the floats my responsibility or the props person?' And I said, 'It could be your responsibility. It could be the props person. It could be the two of you working together. What do you want? What do you feel about that?' It is always about serving whatever the project's needs are, for me. In that sense, I'm thinking very much the way any designer would for the stage: What does this production need?

"There's puppetry in this show and puppetry is something that is of great interest to me. Also, because of my work in film, scale [proportion] is very important. With the puppets I can do work in scale that I cannot do with actors. I can make multiple sizes for the same character. I can have a seven-foot face! It's just a face but it's seven feet tall. Then there are the smaller versions. And the full-size versions. I can't do that with actors. I can do it on film but not with live actors.

"Object theatre is related to puppets. Object theatre is a form in itself. I have elements of object theatre in my work. The floats are object theatre. They are things that have an integrity in and of themselves, they are not just props. They have their own worlds. Each float [in this production] has its own little world. There's one show I did where I had a huge black triangle, as high as the set. It came across the stage at one point and all the lights went to silhouette and the actors froze. Cut into the triangle was the phrase *tempus fugit*, lit from inside. This was about the twilight of empire, the twentieth century and the surrender of the Dutch West Indies to the Japanese. The object takes center stage. It's not the actor, not a performer. It's the object.

"There's the foreground and then there's the background where the shadow puppet work is taking place. It's three-dimensional. What is the relationship of the background to the foreground? I need to tie it together visually. I say that because I came out of dance; my sense of space is more like a dance space but puppet shows are not that at all. I've used puppets from the very beginning of my career. In 1998 I did my first large-scale puppet show. Because I come from visual arts, the control you get with puppets is closer to my roots. They are very set heavy, very technical. Generally when I have a show with people the space is spare. Even if there is a set, it is spare. Because movement is a big part of my vocabulary.

"My aesthetic is clean, it's formal. I have a strong sense of ritual. My roots in film [are] also important; how an image is framed is very important to me. I enjoy working on the stage. I want some relationship to [my art] that's more personal, that's more direct. I'm a first-generation American. I have American elements in me. I have Chinese elements in me. But my identity doesn't have to be answered with a nationality.

"There is no script yet on this new piece I'm working on. There is no script at all. After reading all this [material], I begin to see what images there are. Incredibly there is very little visual imagery available that I could find. But you get the images from the source, from the research. This project has been very hard for me. It's been years of working on it. Three years of research. I've never done so much reading as I have on this project. I went to Brussels and did museum work. There are three narratives: the shadow play, which is from *The Heart of Darkness* [Joseph Conrad], the live part which is the David and Goliath story, using images and ideas from human rights activists, plus the third part, which crosses that, the three-dimensional onstage part, the metanarrative, addressing issues of representation and perception. There is a limited amount of time to do the show; can we do all those things? Can the audience retain the information? It is about essentializing and not saying too much.

"This piece is about representation: Who is representing whom? And determining whose image is included. So that determines at this point how the show begins. It begins with a black-and-white photograph in an African village in the Congo. The photograph is of an African photographing someone and the village is watching him but the kids in the foreground are looking at the other photographer [the one recording this moment]. That's how the show begins. I do a voice-over about the gaze and the gazer. That's what it's really about.

"The linear element in this show is *The Heart of Darkness*. It starts the show. But the middle is not linear. I may jump back and forth in time. It's not just going from *A* to *Z*. The juxtaposition of the past and the present becomes a different medium and then you begin to see relationships in a way you might not if it had been just linear. I've done two puppet shows. They've been based on traditional Japanese ghost stories. They're linear stories but the juxtaposition of the three adds up to something different. Naturalism may suggest a linear [progression] but that's not my way of seeing things. It's not how things really are. I may be talking at this moment but my mind is in many directions. I think of nonlinear as being truer to our way of experiencing reality."

It's Spun Sugar

Daniel Wallace
Independent Scenic Designer, Industrials

Industrials are staged events designed to introduce a new product, a new corporate image, or sustain sales and growth through rallylike meetings of employees. Industrials as a category can include special events and showrooms. They can take place in theatre spaces, rental halls, or hotel convention ballrooms. The Milliken and Company event (a staged presentation of the textiles and chemical manufacturer) had a long history of employing theatre designers and performers for its very theatrical New York industrial presentations. Daniel Wallace began his career by studying theatre design.

"I do industrials and some television. Ninety percent of my work is industrials, mainly pharmaceuticals and product launches and business meetings. I came to New York and began with drafting jobs, assistant work for theatrical productions. I have a degree in theatrical design. Theatre in New York had closed down when I got there. There were maybe four people doing everything because the money had gotten so bad. I came in and did two off-off-Broadway shows. They were horrible experiences. I had more money to spend when I was doing community theatre in Ohio.

"It dawned on me that jobs like that would only get me jobs like that. So I got a call to do drafting for Imero Fiorentino Associates and I took it. They had gone from doing television to full production work including industrials. They had done the Milliken show for years. They were also getting into architectural lighting and studio design. They began hiring costume and set designers. That first year we worked on Miss America, Miss Universe, and the Republican National Convention. These were really big shows. This was work that had never been explained to us in school. I felt guilty that I wasn't doing theatre but the money and the work were great. Almost every job I've gotten since has been because of those early connections. The experience at Fiorentino was like the best graduate school."

Wallace describes how he continues to work with groups of people he met in those early days.

"There is a producer of industrials that pharmaceuticals often hire to stage their product introductions. He hires me to design them. This work is really driven by the creative end. The financial comes second. If the creative end wants a herd of elephants, then you have to find a way to make it work budget-wise. When proposals are developed, there is usually a bottom line and a direction [a focus for the presentation]. This then becomes a bid. We spend a lot of our time doing proposal work. This work is usually done with a writer, a producer, and a set designer. The larger creative team comes on later. By that point we have presented, usually, a white model [a scale model of the set without color—mainly to suggest the larger dimensions and form of the proposed set design] and a budget to the client. The producer I work with most often came from a design background. He is very specific about what he wants. I don't have to spend a lot of time doing sketches trying to guess what he wants. In our first meetings now we usually click right away and I begin with presenting a rough sketch.

"In industrials design, access to the client is very controlled. There is a salesperson and a production company between you and the client. Creative decisions are handed down to me through the production company. This means the producer [of the production company] will stand behind me. He has already had a meeting with the client, and the dates and parameters of the show have been set. The points they want to make have already been established. If it's a business meeting or a product being launched, there is still a corporate message that comes out as an overriding theme for the event. Nothing is ever done without a corporate message. But the producer or creative director is aware of this and usually has given some thought to a direction or approach to the event. When I meet with them, they will talk about what the aims of the meeting or event are, where the meeting or event will take place, a ballroom in a hotel in Florida, for example. There is usually a set of specs [like blueprints] of the performance space at this early meeting. I don't get too crazed here about the dimensions, except I do need to know width and height, especially the height of the ceiling.

"When we discuss concepts at these meetings it is usually around major themes. These recur throughout industrials: 'Go for it.' 'Build for tomorrow.' 'We're a team and proud.' There are only so many themes; you are really trying to sell something, either an idea or a product. Visually, themes are a way of wrapping it all together, an overlayer. These run in cycles. Sports themes, news show themes. These drive the scenery, they drive the graphics, and they give a venue for getting out the message. Usually there is not a full script at this point; there is just a treatment, a brief outline. Sometimes I will get, 'We want an anchor position; there will be two screens, and a conversation area like an interview area. Make it work.' The more I work with specific producers or creative directors, the easier it becomes. We use a kind of shorthand to talk. Sometimes there are small sketches, notes, and pieces of dialogue. But this is not like a theatrical piece where the script is the soul. The key in this work is the corporate image, the corporate message. I always try to find something that hooks me in, maybe a color, fabric, or a finish. Maybe it's brick and steel but heightened. I need this hook. Usually it will come in these early meetings. I can't second-guess the creative director. I have to start with something. Someone once told me, 'Kid, you can always tell from the first production meeting if it's going to work.' If you're clear and you click, you'll get it. If you have to constantly go back and massage it, you're probably not going to get it. It becomes labored and is not spontaneous. This has proven true for me. My first design is usually my best design.

"When I do camera industrials [where the manufacturer is presenting a new camera], I'm basically doing interiors that are propped [have props]. What I'm trying to do is offer an interior design that will show off how well the cameras work. This forces me to work in a smaller scale than I would normally do for a big show. What the manufacturers want is: the colors on the set [should] reproduce on the camera screens as identical. There are about twelve colors with today's cameras that will do that. We still have to be careful of some reds and some purples. This will always be a problem because cameras are an electronic solution for an optical problem. This means the palette I use for this work is usually primaries and gray.

"When I work on the bigger shows, I see one of my jobs as giving the lighting designer a larger canvas on which to work. It becomes all about surfaces and ways to color them with light and then change those colors. It's not about architectural detail. It's about what you see when you walk into the room and how you can change that with lighting. While white is too harsh for video work, I use a light gray, a TV white, and I apply this to basic shapes that are well proportioned on the stage; however, we create that.

"This work is only about thirty years old. We've gone from doing glorified slide shows to video. We could introduce movement into the slides, cross-fade them, scale up or down, but they were still dead images. We needed video to animate the whole thing. Now we can even project the video images on the scenery. We've become technologically driven. There is a pressure to do something different and more spectacular. But of course the budget always stays the same. So as a designer you are always squeezed. It becomes about six basic shapes. Next year we'll do circles. What fascinates me about this work is it becomes about pure design. You are not tied to a script, even though you are tied to the logistics of where people can move when they can enter or exit. The design is driven by what works on a graphic, visual scale. This is very appealing to me.

"Most of the work is in ballrooms. The problem here is that they are never big enough. The carpets are ugly. The ceilings are too low. There aren't enough rigging points in the ceilings. The chandeliers don't do anyone any good because they turn them down for dinner and they are still in the way. Most hotels have freight elevators. That is good, but there's always something to deal with. It's like television studios, 'Where's the sink? How can you have a studio without running water?'

"The same is true with makeup rooms and storage space and sight lines. If the space seats more than 1,000 then you will need video screens that are at least 10½ by 14. It's all video now. It's not so important physically seeing the person onstage, but the audience must see them on the screens, so the screens need to be big enough. Then the question becomes: Is the screen part of the scenery? Does it stand alone? Is there one screen or two? Will there be screen surrounds [scenery that frames the screens]? The real questions for me are how many screens, the size of the screens, the position of the podium if there is one, and how many people need to be onstage at any one time. These become the parameters I have to design around.

"So many designers worry about the request for steps in the front of the stage, but this doesn't worry me. You never see them. There's a sea of heads that blocks out this part of the stage. Remember, this part of the design business was originally handled by [window] display people, not theatre people. Steps are important in terms of size, not visual distraction. Display people would design steps with eight-inch treads and ten-inch risers. This verges on making people trip. You can get by with it if there are only three or four steps, but after that you begin to trip. I go to twelve-inch treads and six-inch risers. This is really about capturing the old theatrical laws. This ratio of step to riser has been known around the theatre forever; it's an architectural law.

"After I talk with the creative director or producer, I go away and work on a ground plan. I do need a plan of the space so I can do a rough estimate of seating to make sure people can fit; what becomes backstage space and space for the projectors. I give this ground plan and the front elevations to the director or producer. Sometimes I do perspective but usually I get the okay on just the elevations. Then I may do a model, in color, usually quarter- to half-inch scale. I usually do these myself, though I may bring in someone to help finish them, color them, and so on. Usually I will do the designer elevations and details. Then tech drawings will go to the shop and come under the supervision of the technical director. I won't see the work again until it comes off the loading truck for the show. If it's a heavy paint show, I may try to send an assistant to the shop to check it out but usually the client doesn't want to spend this kind of money. Because of the time factor and the budget,

I will usually try to get a shop close to the venue. A week in transit [for the scenery] could spell disaster for the work schedule.

"This is all a prep for the final run of the show for the client before the performance. It may cost a lot to do this, but it saves in the end because everyone sees what they're getting. I can do the models very quickly, actually quicker than I can sketch. The level of sketch work in this business has become so detailed, so photo-realistic, that I can't compete with that way of presenting. I prefer to do the models. And I'm well known for my model work. Sometimes I photograph the models for other levels of communicating.

"Conceptually, if I have the time, at least three or four days, I can come up with new ideas and a framing device for the event. If it has to be quick and dirty—I did a show recently in Paris that gave me only four hours—I have to rely on old standbys. But I still have the job, as the designer, to come up with something that works. It depends on the time frame. I bill on a day basis, a day being ten hours long. At the development stage, it could be two hours one day and six hours the next. Most designers do this because we are doing more than one project at the same time. I probably do between fifteen and eighteen projects a year. Most of this work is at conventions or regional meetings, and usually always in ballrooms.

"In terms of design elements, color—or the lack of it—is really important. Geometric shapes are really important because it's that first impression that counts and then too, what the budget will allow. It has to be broad stroked. That means shape and line. How can we pull the focus to the speaker or the screens? What I design is always practical. There's always enough room for the podium, the stairs are at the right place and the right size; these are people coming up on a stage maybe once a year so there's a comfort level and a safety level to consider. How many people need to be onstage? These are the parameters I work with.

"Once I have these decisions in place, the 'design' work can begin. Others tell me my work is very well proportioned. Maybe this comes from my father and his architectural background. I will usually sketch in one-quarter scale and this may help with the proportioning also. The look is usually very nontextured. It is slick surfaces. This is usually more appealing to the client. It's about surfaces and how they play on each other. I did a Tahitian theme recently that did allow for a lot of texture, but then it was painted texture, not dimensional. It's broad strokes. In terms of style, deco is really strong. It's about shapes then, so we have lots of circles and triangles and stairs. These are easily and quickly machineable. 'When in doubt, round the top.' I also like the Memphis-Milan style where I can break up shapes and objects and put them on angles. The appeal of the Memphis style for me was that it was driven by flat colors and shape."

Wallace is referring to the design style of the 1980s that began in Italy and focused on using historical architectural motifs in new combinations to inform industrial and architectural design.

"Most of the staging work is about a thrust design configuration, not about proscenium. The scenery exists behind the stage. We still have to separate the people on stage from the screens and because of the lighting. So it becomes about layers of design—the stairs, the foreground, the podium position, the middle ground, and then the scenery begins, the background. But there is the sense of a simultaneous set; there is no reveal as with a proscenium arch. This is a more presentational style. We still have to deal with the sound and light people, of course. There is always a battle for space, the critical four feet. We sometimes can hide the speakers behind white scrim panels but it is always a task.

"Lighting has become much more complicated today. There are the cyberlights [sometimes called moving lights or intelligent fixtures that work with remote positioning and color changes]. These require more time for hanging, focusing, and programming, usually one full night. This means less time for the scenery work.

"Ultimately, design for industrials is the same as designing for the theatre. The skills are the same. The choices are the same. But it is what's driving those choices that is different. The budgets are different also. The budgets are high and the expectations are high.

"In the old days set designers would be much more involved with the graphics. What goes on the screens with the slides? Now this area of design has become its own world. There are specific designers for the graphics, the animations, and computer-generated images.

"And we have to smoke the room. That means we have to have smoke to punch the cyberlight beams. People don't smoke anymore so the rooms look differently. The lighting reads differently. We try to keep the scenery as simple as we can. There is always the time issue. There is rarely enough time to rehearse, to get stagehands, to rig moving scenery, and so on. We used to have three days to put in, now it's down to two days.

"There is no union jurisdiction for industrials but I do maintain my United Scenic Artists union membership. I do two or three television projects a year.

"The expectations are changing. There is a real sense of the MTV influence. There is a raw, unpolished look currently that is driven by the budgets—they keep getting smaller—and the lack of experience. I don't like it when people say, 'Well it doesn't matter.' It does matter. It matters to me. If we can do it better, we need to.

"My work finally is about communication. It's about ideas being presented. I can still walk into one of the ugliest ballrooms in America and make it look like something. I enjoy the work; we are making magic in our own way. It's not mystical or pretentious. We want people to pay attention to what we have to say. My work has a short life. It lives for maybe a week and then it's gone. You have a very short time to make your point. It's spun sugar."

This Is Not About Velcro

Linda Fisher
Costume Designer
Broadway, film, and video

Linda Fisher has worked as a costume designer on Broadway with A Tuna Christmas, Bus Stop, Morning's at Seven, *and* Painting Churches, *among others. In television she has worked for* Saturday Night Live, ABC, NBC, HBO, PBS, *and* CBS. *She has done miniseries as well as pilots. She has also done costume work for films including* After the Storm *and* Heart of Midnight. *She began her career by studying theatre design. A very successful off-Broadway show,* Greater Tuna *is a two-person comedy written by Joe Sears, Jaston Williams, and Ed Howard. Two actors play some twenty characters over the two acts, and the show is known for the effectiveness and humor of its idiosyncratic characters, their look, and the quick costume changes.*

"I started by designing in the theatre. [At one point] I worked on a PBS film of two Mark Twain stories, *The Private History of a Campaign That Failed* and *The War Prayer*. It was low budget but worth it. For a costume designer the transition is not that difficult. It's not that much different. You need to think in terms of designing for the front row. Most designers will design for the theatre from center of house but the switch is only to the front row. It's just in your mind as you begin to design. There are close-ups and there are distant shots.

"If you are working with real actors concerned about their characters and a real director concerned about the script and your input, not just 'the person who shops for shoes,' then the process is really exciting. It's the kind of collaborative thing that theatre is good at. It's about character, how the script develops. It's about registering the character. Do you want to know everything about the character when you first see him or do you want the audience to be fooled? Do you want to be led astray? Or do you want the audience to be confused by what they see the character wearing? The more film you do with stars, the more the process of design becomes about what the star looks like, not the character. It becomes about the publicity shots and everyone has to look beautiful. It becomes boring to do the pretty people. The characters, real characters, are the interesting work. It is possible to do the beautiful thing, but within character, not the latest mode of fashion.

"There is a time, in the middle of the process of design, when I completely doubt everything. I learned a long time ago that when that happens, you just push it aside and you ignore it completely. And you wait. It's like roulette. Once you place your bets you can't change them. It's part of the rules. And part of the fun. And once you get onstage and all the other elements are added, it usually becomes way more interesting than you thought. It's like the playwright. When they write, more often than not, there's much more in the script than they know. Theatre and film as collaborative art will only work when you have different minds coming together.

"The difference in design for theatre and design for film is in the technicalities, not in the process of design. There is a feeling that 'good' film costume design means the scenery and the clothes match. I find this too awful for words. The key is getting the designers on the same track. If you, as the costume designer, and the set designer or art director are thinking in the same way, you don't have to meet constantly. You say, here's the dress fabric, let me see the couch fabric. If there's a problem one of you has to fix it.

"Too often this sequence of being on the same track is skewed. The theatre or film company gets the set designer, then months later they get a costume designer, then way down the road the lighting designer comes onboard. It is so much better if you can start off thinking at the same time.

"In those early meetings I would find a real difference between film and theatre. I would come in talking about the characters, their through lines and the pacing and the ups and downs of the script, and the others working on the film would get these blank looks. They seemed to wonder, 'Why isn't she out buying the shoes?' They seemed to feel they needed to tell me what color everything should be. This may have started in Hollywood. Some of it had to do with pampering the 'stars' and some had to do with the nature of directors and the production designers.

"You try to make it a positive thing. When *Greater Tuna* [which Fisher designed] was first developed in Hartford, it was one of the greatest experiences in my life. We all met together in my apartment, the actors, the designers, and the director. We spent a whole day just going through the script as it was. Anyone could say anything. We started with the idea that you could see through the characters so I thought about costumes [as transparencies]. The character Didi has a plastic raincoat; this is left over from that early conversation. There were discussions about seeing only parts of an actor or character to address the issue of multiple costume changes. That helped a lot. Maybe we only see the character's feet or the character's head.

"There were early discussions about transferring the stage script to film and video. We did a pilot. The script was rewritten. The question of quick changes was dropped. I could do waist cinchers and we could do makeup changes. This approach had nothing to do with quick changes. And it didn't add to the humor of the piece. The problem was getting the quick-change idea, and the humor of that, into a filmed version. Subsequently, the theatre producer taped the show over several performances and edited it down. There was also some pickup work with close-ups. This means you have the quality of the stage, the quick-change thing, and the visual gag of these two guys playing all the parts, and the audience reactions.

"I tried to think of the play as being one day. This made the costume changes easier. There are some changes there but the time is shorter. I also wanted to keep the characters apart with color. I wanted each character to have their own color. One character, Bertha, is always in some version of green. Sometimes it's a lime green, sometimes a brighter green. The character of Vera, I thought of as the prom queen. She is always in peach. Sometimes the ruffles are too big or the slip is showing and she doesn't know it. She wears knee-highs and when she sits down the line is there. There are cracks in the façade. If the actor comes back in a different costume, though still the same character, have I confused the audience? There is little time for this.

"A lot of the costumes have padding built into them to shift the body silhouette. And then there is the question of fastening. If you take the costume off quickly there can be one kind of fastening device. If you are putting it on quickly, another. This is not about Velcro. Then you ask, 'How many things can the actor keep on underneath?' Sometimes it's easier to put on two pairs of pants and peel one off rather than have the actor change pants. There are two to three dressers for each show. It's frantic. The actors are actually carrying on a conversation, the dialogue, while they are doing the quick changes. This means they are miked. So now I have to deal with that issue as well.

"I think you cannot teach design. It's either in you or it isn't. Studying design can help you make it happen. I have a friend who's a painter and she will comment on something like the use of color. And I go, 'My God, I never thought of that.' But I think somewhere I have. I do the sketches, I do the drawings with paint and such, I do the fittings and the shopping. And then, when I'm finished, I'll go back and say, 'Oh, there is a pattern there.' But I haven't thought about it consciously. It's just there. I realize the ingénue and the male lead are in the same blue color but if I had thought about it before it would be too self-conscious, too pedantic.

"I work through process—my process. I start doing research, then drawings, then shopping for fabric. I can't paint at this point, because if I do the perfect fabric in paint I won't find it. If I shop [for fabric] as part of the process, I'll usually find something that's way better than anything I could have imagined. Even if it's modern wear, I'll try to shop as the character. So it's subjective design. And it all comes from the script. When I first read a script I'm trying to get down the technicalities of it.

"How many changes will there be? The basics. What time of year, of day? I did a production of Molière's *The Bungler* at the Long Wharf Theatre and the first reading was critical. I get a lot from first readings. I discovered real problems there with the quick changes for the *masquers*. I try never to skip the first reading. Suddenly you have a face and a voice. And an actor and a character personality. You don't want to get too far in your first impressions when you read the script alone. When you see the cast it could be totally different. Are you going to go with the way the person looks, the actor, or are you going with the way you first thought it should be?

"When you read the script by yourself, you make all the lists. Sometimes I start by just reading the script for the story. Then I read it again for the technicalities. 'Oh, he comes off here and comes back later.' If I get sent a script ahead of time, I try to come in like I know the script and can at least talk about it intelligently. Sometimes I do all this work and then never get the job. But that's a part of the business.

"Some of this first talk is selling yourself. But then even a fitting is a selling job. You are selling the costume to the actor. And being a psychologist. This seems to be more true of costume design, less so with set design or lighting design. You are the confidante, the sales person. If the show is modern, I try to bring several choices for the actor. I've found that if you bring the 'one perfect choice,' the choice is between that thing and everything else that's out there. That can be time-consuming. If I bring several items, the choice is usually between those offered. You think something will work but you really don't know until it's on the person. It may seem to me to work for the character but whether it works for the actor as that character—I don't know until they put it on.

"There are still technical issues with choices. If something is going to be videotaped or filmed and then transferred to video, patterns and colors, for example, are an issue. Red flares; patterns that are similar and close to each other create problems. Anything that is of close but contrasting value is a problem. White flares.

"The first film I worked on was under time pressures. We met one day and began shooting the next. I did a kind of costume parade for the director of the main characters. The only thing he was worried about was blue, which he thought would be too bright. I didn't have to dye down any of the whites. I sometimes hate seeing everything 'teched' down. There is a tech dye you can buy for film and video work. You put everything white in the dye bath and it makes everything this kind of tan and that makes it work for the camera. But I find if you are working with a really good DP [director of photography], then white can be wonderful sometimes. If it's a medical show, you may want the medical technicians to be in white, not tan. Sometimes when a shot is being set up, you may notice something not working, then you do have to make some adjustment. It's my problem finally. It's part of the collaboration. It's my job to notice if something is not working. And you're always learning. It's always new.

"Collaboration is a complicated process. Sometimes you want to blame the director for not giving you enough. But you have to remember that your job is to create, to offer something. And always the authority dynamics are drawn differently. Sometimes you use the set design to get to the director. Or you and the actor go to the director. Or you and the director go to the actor. Sometimes you have something you think is fabulous and everyone else hates it. And you wonder why. Or you want desperately to change something and everyone says no, leave it. The designs keep changing all the time. If someone asks me, 'Have you got a design yet?' I say no. It's not finished until the show is up and running. You are designing at the beginning. You are designing in early rehearsals. You are designing in fittings. You are designing in a dress rehearsal. It also has to do with the people you are working with. If someone can do beautiful beadwork then that's what you do. If you design a strong character statement and the actor gives up too soon and says, 'I can't work with that,' then the design is compromised. Maybe all it needs is a little time.

"I think all costume designers should be onstage at least once in a costume. The actor is developing a character and a vision. The costume design has done the same thing. Sometimes the timelines are different. And designers can get into ruts easily. You start responding automatically. You read a sitcom script and you go, 'Oh, yeah, I know that character type and I'll do this . . .' Whether you go to museums or just walk up and down the streets of New York, you get more stuff to use. I keep books of photography with wonderful people in them. When you start to work on a project, you start looking. It may be random, but then you see one tiny thing, something that will set you off on a direction. You may leave that little tiny thing behind, but it set you off on the direction."

Confetti in the Sky

Jean McFaddin
Marketing and Events Consultant

The Macy's Thanksgiving Day parade began in 1924. It was first broadcast nationally on television in 1948 by NBC. The parade currently draws over two million people along the full parade route in New York. Another sixty million viewers watch the televised broadcast. The latest additions to the parade balloons include both video game characters and Internet characters. Jean McFaddin was parade director between 1977 and 2001. As Senior Vice President for Public Relations and Events at Macy's East, she was also responsible for the annual fireworks show celebrating the Fourth of July. She began her studies in theatre.

"After I left college I went into regional theatre as a director, doing 'traditional theatre.' I went into my first job as a costume designer because that was the job available. I really wanted a job as a director, but since I cared about the whole process of theatre making, this gave me a chance to work in the theatre and, I now realize, gave me the chance also to look at the full workings of the theatre. I was, even then, really a producer.

"Of course, I wanted to come to New York, like most theatre people of my generation, and the opportunity to do so was as a producer. I served as the artistic director of the James Joyce Liquid Theatre. Looking back, I realize I was actually functioning as, thinking as, and gaining interest as a producer. Because of the avant-garde nature of the Liquid Theatre, there was real interest generated in Europe, and this finally led to opportunities with festivals. I never really wanted to deal with the proscenium theatre anyway; I was always interested in new forms. My regional theatre experiences were either with theatre-in-the-round or thrust stages and the idea of public events and festivals tapped that interest. Festivals were 'beyond the round.' Like the Liquid Theatre, they involved the audience much more. Looking back, the key for me was getting away from the proscenium and involving the audience.

"The national bicentennial celebrations led to the city of New York land festivals, part of which was the fireworks display for the Statue of Liberty. The Disney Corporation was then doing this, but Macy's was the official sponsor. I met my counterpart then and, as it happened, she left Macy's. But they had seen my work and they called me. The joke was I thought they were calling to offer me a credit card. But they had bigger plans. I was offered the job as in-house producer of special events.

"At this time the chairman of the board at Macy's, Edward Finkelstein, was redefining the public events Macy's had been sponsoring as 'theatre in retail.' His business acumen and insights meshed with my own background experiences. The Thanksgiving Day parade was a part of this rethinking. The parade had been mainly an in-house event for employees. It did not have the scope or coverage it now has. The fireworks, Santa, especially the references to the film, *Miracle on 34th Street*, the flower show, these together with the parade offered real opportunities for growth and development. The real challenge was: How do you take all these icons, these Macy's events, and bring them back to life? And how do you afford to do that?

"My second mandate was a personal one. I realized that my own evolving sense of what makes theatre work was audience-centered. Too many people were, and are, making a kind of theatre that is about them. It becomes about the process of doing theatre and what the director, the designers, and the actors get out of it. But that's not what it's about at all. It's about what the audience gets out of it. Theatre for me was always about the experience. It is about what the audience learns from the experience. It can be emotional, yes, but it is also educational. This means the audience must be given the chance to participate, to be a part of the experience. This seems to me the same in film. The final objective is both emotional and education, to feel something and to learn something. For me the parade brought all of this thinking together. The parade is a tradition. It's about family and Thanksgiving. About coming together. For most of the audience the parade is a television experience, not a live experience. Two million may see it live but forty-eight to sixty million people see it on television. So it is a public experience, a television experience, and an employee experience. Because of course it's the employees who do the parade.

"It was a great celebration, a great American holiday, and a great American experience. After I figured out what the parade was, the same way I used to break down the script and figure out what the play was, I had to relate those parts. You have to define the structure first, then define what you are doing, even if it's to break the boundaries. The boundaries of my work gave me the structure.

"So I had to define what the experience of the parade was. It had a professional side and an amateur side. The employees and their families were a major component. Having come out of regional theatre, I loved the idea, again, of people working together, volunteering for an event—helping. The parade recreated that forum for me, the group experience.

"But the parade needed a good script. It needed to respond to the visual nature of the parade. The balloons were old and in bad shape. The floats were too similar, the same style, the same size. So I said, 'What's wrong with this picture?' The answer was, 'You have a lot of floats on the ground, one size, and then you jump way up in the air with the balloons and there is nothing in between.' We're going from A to Z with a void in the middle. We needed to fill that void. A parade is like confetti. The magic of confetti is when you throw it up—you get all the different colors, all the different sizes, and all the different angles. You get clumps; you get scatters. What does confetti look like in the sky?

"Answering that question meant working on the visual picture for the parade. I needed more variety of size, of shape, of color. What is the 'line of march' [the order of the parade]? The improvisation of the parade is how do you put all these pieces together, in what order, to create the most exciting pictures? And celebrity helps create the excitement. It's much more exciting to see your favorite cartoon character, a Bugs Bunny balloon for example, than to just see a rabbit balloon.

"And then there was size. Before you have big, you have to have small. You need the contrast. So I introduced the ornamental balloons to fill the in-between spaces, to give variety and a sense of changing scale. This makes the bigger balloons look really bigger. I also needed to introduce variety in the floats. There needed to be more animation, more contrast. And the floats could introduce entertainment. I began to look at it as 'the longest running show on Broadway.' The parade was unique because it was on Broadway. So shouldn't it feature not only celebrities, but also Broadway talent? So we needed to create 'stages' or spaces for the performers to present on. Otherwise it was just about people riding by and waving. The question was: 'How do you make the floats perform?' You animate them. And you set up stages for the performers. The parade had to become a great piece of theatre entertainment.

"The line of march needs a heartbeat, the sound of the bands and the music. The movement of color and sound, everything coming together; a kind of cacophony. This needs to be spread out more, to create key moments. The floats are more immediate, they're theatre. You need to get that moment. The balloons are 'awe'. You want that 'awe' factor. You need contrasts, though, breaks within. It can't just all be about the clowns and laughter.

"The actual parade can be more about the sustained impressions but the televising of the parade needs more control. It is a more intense and controlled experience. It needs highs and lows. It is a different medium. There is no longer the advantage of scale. Everything on television is the same scale. The camera edits what you see. This affects my decisions about the line of march. You have to prioritize with the television broadcast crew. What will be seen more often, what will get more attention? For television the clowns become the confetti. You see a little of them, multicolored. They keep hopping in and out. The clowns will do actual routines on the street level for the audience but not on camera.

"The television imposes a different time sequence. Commercials change the rhythm and the flow. On the street the rhythm keeps building and building to the final climax . . . and it's Santa Claus! On television the flow is more little acts or scenes punctuated by the commercials. But there still needs to be variety and build just as with a play. The television allows for full performances, whole sequences performed for the camera, not just the partial moments as the acts pass by.

"So the parade really is three events. It is a great employee event [for Macy's]. It is a great public event [for New Yorkers] and it is a great television event [for a national audience]. Each of these required something different, something to be treated. Each needed to complement and support the other.

"The producer half of me needed to find the partnerships that would allow for raising funds to improve and expand the parade. These partnerships led more and more to the celebrity characters. We can't just put in Mickey Mouse or Kermit the Frog. That is a character with certain protections. People own the rights to these characters. So to not only get the right to use these characters, but to get the owners to pay for the right to have them in the parade was the real challenge. We had to create the world's greatest stage that stars were willing to pay to be in.

"One strategy was to keep all the stars on equal footing. There was very little hierarchy, except perhaps for Santa Claus. There is no grand marshal as in other parades. We decided to make Santa Claus the grand marshal; nobody after all can compete with Santa Claus and that put everyone else on the same level. There was no one star.

"There was real competition early on between the production of the parade and the television coverage. My position was to create a great parade and a great television show. To emphasize one over the other was to shoot myself in the foot. One had to enhance the other. Big stars got exposure through the television coverage. But the live parade is the topic of the coverage.

"Part of the rethinking of this parade was adding the 34th Street segment, the city's longest block from Broadway to 7th Avenue. The block is so long you are able to have two giant balloons at the same time within view. No other section of the parade route allows for this. And this new block included 12,000 new live audience members. It became like a three-ring circus. And you never leave one of the rings empty. [The ring in front of Macy's is more proscenium staging.] The public nature of the parade does not prevent anyone from televising the parade at certain points. We created an exclusive point for NBC by creating an exclusive staging area in front of the store. In that 'zone' no other camera crews are allowed. The talent is prepared and we can rehearse sequences specifically for camera coverage.

"The parade is about things continuing to move forward. The television show is different. It is about being in the heart of the parade. Routines are created for this 'zone.' Camera shots are planned for this moment. This becomes exclusive to NBC.

"The overriding organizational strategy is that the parade is for children, and by extension, for their families. The content should be appropriate to that audience. And then the parade needed an organizational theme. There are thematic segments to the parade. There is the Americana section, the children's section, the action section, and, of course, the ending section, which is Santa Claus. Originally, this was one of the hardest things to deal with in the parade. You start off with Thanksgiving as the theme and then end up with Christmas. How do you get from one holiday to another? And then you have to consider how the television audience changes as the parade progresses. It usually starts with children watching and then adults coming in later. We wanted to start with something magic that the children would love. Then we had performances from Broadway shows to help pull in that adult audience.

"You also have to balance the balloon characters. We realized one year the parade was going, literally, 'to the dogs.' We had Snoopy, Clifford, Blue, and Beethoven. Every time you looked up in the sky there was a dog, because dogs were so popular.

"There are also real decisions about the details of the balloons. There is color, size. First and foremost is aerodynamics. Will it fly well? Is it a popular character, identifiable? Does it add variety and interest or is it just a repetition?

"I think, really, I've been doing theatre all the time I've been doing the parade. The same is true with the fireworks. I was trained to put real importance on the visuals in theatre—the set, the costumes, and all the other elements. The elements of the spectacle. Any show I did, I had a picture of that show in my head. When I moved to events work that was a great plus. I see a picture and break it down into how to get there. I saw the parade in my mind, what it should look like. When I did the fireworks I saw it as a light show, lighting in the sky. Pyrotechnics at first was done without control. But the change in the business, especially with computer control, gave me a chance to create a picture and then program it. Color, timing, variety, the breaks, the size of the charges and explosions. Electrical firing and computer programming allowed greater control. This eliminated the fuse problems. It became more reliable and safer. Now with this level of control we could start really planning a design. We could create choreography.

"Whether it is a flower show, a parade, a fireworks event, a store opening, a pageant, or a play: all of these events have the same sequence. You have to start by visualizing it and then working backward. It's still creating great entertainment, a great show. In theatre one normally works, first, from a script that has been created by an author, that has a message in the world of his characters. As a producer or director you are now working with a known quantity: a play, in a defined time, a defined space, the theatre, a vehicle. If you are a director you are now governed by that script. Your job is to realize the world the author has created. In events, one is not working with that script. One is working with a message, though. You then create the form of the event. Is it going to be a parade? Is it going to be a staged show? How will we do this opening at the mall? Outside? Inside? Where's the best staging area? Where's the best place for the audience? Where can I have the biggest audience?

"Events can be as theatrical as the stage. But there is the freedom from a script. I create my own script for the event. I do start by creating a script, a script of my own. In that sense, the line of march, the order of the parade, is a script. In the theatre the script is the message and creates the experience. In the parade or in events, the description of the elements, the sequence, becomes the dialogue. With the fireworks, the script is really the musical score. If you create a musical score, you give the possibility for interpretation. What I did with the fireworks, which no one had done before, was to create a musical score, a script first. And a good script in this sense needs to be able to stand on its own, just as reading a stage script needs to stand on its own. But when you add the performers, the fireworks, it comes to life.

"I did *Coucou Bazar*, one of the 'practicables' by Jean Dubuffet [French pop artist, 1901–1985]. This influenced me. How the visual canvas-based artist can become dimensional and theatrical. Every element can be moved and the painting becomes new. How do you translate this work to other forms? We took his works; he created new parts, costumed characters coming to life. This is what I later did with the fireworks. Fireworks are like a thousand individual pictures but it becomes the relationship between the pictures that forms the new message. What is the progression of the pictures? There can be individual moments. There can be highs and lows. There can be emotional moments. Proud moments. Touching moments. Or what I call a popcorn moment, a throwaway moment. You can't have only big and expensive moments. There needs to be change and contrast.

"Collaboration is what it is all about. I come from theatre and it's that early training in collaboration, the roles and how they play out, that impressed me. If I had started in another medium, it could have been very different. I see the project through various eyes: the director, the producer, the designer. These were real roles for me. You have to understand the differences in building what I call a partnership. You need to make the group effort, different people with different talents, a whole. The truth is they are all creative. And they deserve your respect. But my sense of collaboration goes even further. I think of the collaboration with the audience. In theatre sometimes we seemed to be playing to the audience. My goal became to play with the audience. This is the ultimate collaboration."

The following three interviews are interrelated by topic. At the time of these interviews, each designer was working on the Xbox game system developed by the Microsoft Corporation. This system is known for detailed graphics and smooth animation comparable to film. Emphasis has been placed on the visual artists in the development of the games. These individuals come from very different backgrounds and preparations, but each is involved in creating a newer language of performance.

Almost Like a Dream

Dave McCoy
GFX Techniques Consultant
Microsoft

"I became interested in CGI, computer-generated imagery. This led me to video games where there were no rules beyond those borrowed from other media. I am now called a Graphics Techniques Consultant. Before this I was called a creative director. I consult with artists to help them improve or realize [their] talent. They supply the message, I don't. I offer ways to achieve the results. This can be specific knowledge of systems or general arts principles. The rules are the same. Here is how they get applied in this medium. Here is how you can achieve results. To work with artists to help them achieve their vision.

"To some degree I try to reassure people who are good artists to practice good art. The principles are consistent regardless of the technology. Let me help, as a consultant, to make the technology almost disappear. The artist can then focus on: 'What is my message? Why am I here? What am I trying to do here? How am I trying to change the emotional state of the viewer? What is it that I am trying fundamentally to communicate here?' And let me help to get the technology out of the way so you can focus on those questions.

"We want to have the viewer feel afraid. Or we want the viewer to become relaxed and feel content. The screen evaporates. Almost like a dream. The distinction between fiction and reality evaporates. The person had this experience. When they remember it, will they remember themselves playing a game or will they go, 'You know if I really had this experience, I would feel as I feel now. I didn't really drive a race car around the track. But I came to this turn and the car started to lose control and I was frightened. And I felt that fear. And then I got to the winner's circle and everyone cheered.' And then I think, if I was really in a race it would probably feel like that. We want to create that in the moment and in the memory.

"[This is] a new approach to storytelling. The audience is on the stage. The audience will join the play. They may choose to be friendly with some of the characters or not. I want conventional drama in this. Just as in film or theatre, I need to make choices in design. I need to analyze the script, the story, and balance the subtle with the obvious to tell the story.

"Usually a game designer will present the ideas. This is not a graphics designer–type role, rather it is the narrative, the components of the story. There is usually a discussion of characters and themes. The game designer will work with an art director, who will choreograph what the key elements of the game are. Here are the locations, if you will. Here are the principal costumes. Here are the relevant props. It cannot always be storyboarded, as in film, but storyboarding is intrinsically sequential. It might be more comparable to Disney designing a theme park. We don't always know where the guests will walk but we can design the environment in which they walk. We expect their gaze to be drawn. The art director and staff artists design this concept for the game. Concept includes the locales, the costumes, the props, and so on. Now the narrative logic is hopefully emerging. This leads to a coordinating team. But a lot of this is still unpredictable. There is a player.

"It's complex enough, and the rules aren't there yet, so people are still learning this medium. It's not just about a game. It can be about new emotional access."

The Adrenaline Factor

Kiki Wolfkill
Art Director-Racing Games
Microsoft

"I began with art history as a background. This has become something of a reference point in my current work with racing and sports game design. Art history is very important. I need to see how others have expressed [the range] of human emotions. This can feed my work. Generations of artists have expressed the same ideas I'm dealing with; I need to learn from them. Color and how light gets rendered are critical to the realization of our game environment. I have found too few artists who can render new textures, not just the ones available in existing software programs. This means finding people who can see, who look at the world every day.

"My work needs to be collaborative, with the producer and the programmer as well as my staff of designers. I want to create a world for the game player that is challenging, unique, and unexpected. There are dark ride games and fantasy games but our work is about the rush of anticipation. Ironically, as the software and hardware become more powerful and process more quickly, the expectations rise. The possibilities for realistic representation become greater, as does the expectation of the game player. We have to be careful that we do not become just more realistic. We have to find ways to increase the adrenaline factor more creatively.

"At times it's important to just let the technology go. It will come back when you need it.

"I have certain expectations: style and personality cannot get lost. We have to find those design elements that create the sense of an inclusive environment. Racing games, for example, have to deal with the horizon line but they also have to create the sense of movement, as the horizon line changes. The [newer] urban landscapes, cityscapes, created for racing games afford more opportunity for the illusion of speed, quick movement, and that adrenaline rush."

The Elephant Is One

J.D. Alley
Art Director
Leisure, Imagination, and Family Entertainment
Microsoft Corporation

"I began my career studying painting, searching for content. I realized that I was a good draftsman and illustrator, but [then realized] I had nothing to say. I walked away from being creative and did some other things. I worked as a principal storyboard artist and production designer. There's no place to go to study to be a storyboard artist. You either have the sense of it or you don't. You understand what a DP [director of photography] and a director want. You begin to think like they think. You take their words and do fifteen pages of storyboards for the next day. The half-life for storyboards for film is one day. The process of storyboards crystallizes the thinking of the project. This was where I developed the idea of 'If the elephant is one.'

"The skills of the mechanical process of design lacked continuity. This is systemic in our business. We are tool-centric. So we began by saying, 'What's the single more important thing about this environment?' That becomes the elephant, the coherent unit."

Alley is referring to the old story, a Hindu fable, of the elephant being described by a group of blind people, where each has experienced only one part of the elephant. Those who felt the trunk described the elephant as a snake. Those who touched the legs described the elephant as a tree trunk. Those who felt the tail described the elephant as a hippopotamus. Those who touched the ears described the elephant as a sail. No one had been able to piece the parts together, to see the whole.

"Everything else has to relate to the choice about the environment—every design choice. Once the elephant is clear, that is, once the choice is made about the environment, all other choices become easier. Is the scale wrong? Is the palette wrong? Is the voice wrong? The reference point is still the elephant, the principal choice in designing the environment. I have something now in this subjective world of choices that seems more objective. When you are doing collaborative, subjective work, the hardest thing to do is getting everybody to see the same thing simultaneously. This is one reason designers are useful.

"What I really am is an art manager. There is a technical lead that manages technical development of the software. There is a test lead who manages all the internal testing of the games developed. There are project managers who manage the process of the development of the project. The art lead is finally responsible for the visual design and execution of the game. All of a sudden words like *production designer, cinematographer, lighting designer, set designer, costume designer*, all of those things now matter to us. They never mattered before. They matter now. We now have the technology to create new art forms.

"Historically this work has been driven by the technology with precious little thought given to creating entertainment. Our industry has misunderstood our contract [our expectation with our customers]. What we sell is a time experience. We don't sell games . . . we sell time . . . transcendent time. It changes the way the clock runs for us individually. Now we have to look at what is uniquely different about us [computer games] and television or film or books or the theatre. It is a first-party, interactive experience. Instead of watching the movie, you can be the movie.

"There is a body of syntax that informs most viewers. We know for example about P.O.V. [point of view]. If the camera is moving stealthily through the alleyway, we instinctively know that it is the bad guy. We know the language. We do the translation.

"The best games are like morality plays. They are, fundamentally, about good and evil—the consequences of choices, good and evil. The choice needs to really matter.

"Historically, I was limited. I was limited in the number of polygons I could use. I was limited in the number of textures I could use. But if the technology is the sole driving force, then the technological concerns outweigh the story. Suddenly artists want not only to create a doorway, but also to create the realistic hinges, a digital artifact. We need instead to have a conversation about the door. Do you want to get out of the room? What do you want to accomplish? We spend too much time and money on building a door that's never going to open. Not only that, we build a backside to the door that we are never going to see. I can take two polygons and a very clever texture map and make you believe that door really opens.

"The design elements are not different. The models are there from the other media. We need to now look at the canvas. We don't talk about the director yet, the director of photography, or the production designer. We have been so focused on just the technology doing what we wanted it to do. My feeling is that the use of design for this medium should be no different than that for other media. We need to be more like John Singer Sargent the painter, less photorealism. The illusion of life is more powerful [than] some factual depiction.

"Right now we want you to see the craft. We are proud of what we can do. We have to now [move to the next stage] and make that craft invisible. The job is to support the narrative. It has to be about the passion of the gesture, the message of the work.

"It's a great time to be a writer, a performer, a visual artist. Collaboration is the challenge."

The Seats Have to Go

Eugene Lee
Scenic Designer
Broadway, television, film

In addition to several nominations, Eugene Lee has won two Tony awards for his Broadway designs for Candide *and* Sweeney Todd. *His theatrical design work on Broadway also includes* Ragtime *(Tony award nomination),* Agnes of God, A Moon for the Misbegotten, On the Waterfront, *and* Showboat. *He also received Tony nominations for* The Changing Room *and* The Sunshine Boys. *For film he has designed* Vanya on 42nd Street, Mr. North, Hammett, Easy Money, *and* Gilda Live, *among others. He is the production designer for NBC's Saturday Night Live. Lee studied theatre design in school.*

"I'm working [now] on two projects. And they are both kind of interesting but both kind of different in terms of what's happening with them. They are *Bounce* for Harold Prince [the producer and director] and Stephen Sondheim [the composer, lyricist]. Prince called and said he was looking for a 'big idea,' a big theatrical framework for the whole thing. This was something we had worked on before, like the factory in *Sweeney Todd*, which had nothing really to do with [the story] but was a frame [for that story]. The other project, *Wicked*, with a different director, Joe Mantello (*Vagina Monologues* and *Love! Valour! Compassion!*), who is far more interested in what the show would look like."

Bounce is loosely based on the Addison Meisner biography. Wicked *is based on the Gregory Maguire book* Wicked: The Life and Times of the Wicked Witch of the West, *a Stephen Schwartz musical (*Pippin, Godspell, Children of Eden*).*

"I'm working with Joe right now on *Wicked*. And he was an actor before he was a director. And he's so interested in what [the set] will look like. They are all so interested in 'what it will look like' and I want to go, 'You know, we'll know when we [first] figure out the play.' It's just storytelling. This is not complicated. This is not scrim. Simple.

"This is the same issue [for me] with *Wicked*. It has so many scenes and is written well but like a movie. And there's no [information yet] in the script about how to do it. Example: There's a famous scene in the movie, and now in this musical, but not the same; where Dorothy melts the witch. The scarecrow is with us. She grabs a bucket of water and she tosses it on the scarecrow and it gets on the witch and she melts. An important scene and very dramatic. And in this musical, and because of its kind of backward view, the good witch is watching all this happen. One basic premise here is that the witches were best friends in school. So the scene becomes also about seeing your friend assassinated. They had grown apart and weren't friends anymore but then when people you've loved turn on you, it's the worst hurt of all. Which, in a way, is what this musical is about. But of course at this point the script is [providing] no hope at all [for how to stage the scene]. It just says, 'there's a handy torch nearby.' Oh, yeah, sure. They're everywhere!

"So here we are. You know this musical is a kind of a domestic version of the movie. It's the life of the Wicked Witch of the West, how she grew up. Her troubles because she's green. It's more like about roommates. They are tossed together. Glenda comes from a wealthy, well-to-do family. And here she is with this roommate who was born green, doesn't have any money. There's a real situation here. They become close, become friends, and then grow apart for lots of reasons and they end up on opposite ends of the spectrum. And here we are at an important scene at the end of the musical and this character is melted, is killed.

"And so you say, 'How are we going to do that?' 'Let's think about this.' 'What would help the actors here?' So we said to ourselves, 'It's the laundry.' We didn't want to see the witch melt. That can only happen in the movie; we wanted to see it in some kind of abstract way. Like maybe a silhouette. The scene will be very simple, okay? It'll be an antique washing machine, a bucket, a caldron sitting on a big fire. And up and down the stage—the cheapest thing in the world, no money—just lines of laundry. Because after all it's the castle's laundry so there could be a lot of laundry. Not just one sheet to telegraph [the information] but socks and shirts and lots of clothes. And then the famous four can come from way in the back of the set, through a door, through the laundry, and when they get downstage there's this confrontation that results in the melting, as a shadow, a silhouette. This is how I think. When you work with different people you have to find out how they work.

"In *Wicked* what got me going was it was so complicated. The writer is working like [it is] a movie or television. And he says, 'Suddenly a kitchen from the past appears.' This is a flashback to explain how she was born. And I say, okay, I know how to do this. We'll do it like a pageant wagon, from the past. Medieval theatre. In the [Gregory Maguire] novel there is a lot of talk about the witch. If you read it, if you look at the lyrics, sooner or later there will be something that gives you a clue. You have to find out what the witch was really like. She is a famous character like Princess Diana or Jackie Kennedy but what were they really like? There's all this history and we can do this simply, theatrically. It will be simple then. The audience will wonder 'Is this a reenactment?' 'Is it really happening?' It's left kind of vague. How do I do this flashback to the past? How do I move it along fast? Very simple, the Eugene way.

"I made an effort when I talked with the producers: If I understand it, I'll do it. I had just finished the anniversary show for *Saturday Night Live*. Joe Mantello was looking for a designer for *Wicked*. This is a great idea. It's kind of mean. I called the scene shop that built *Ragtime* and lots of [other] things for me. Ironically, they had just finished building a set for a regional production of an Oz musical with big flowers. And [when I heard that] I said you've got to do my set, it's all black and mean and kind of interesting and personal—the other side of [Oz]. In my musical, the yellow brick road is built by animal slave labor. I mean, when a house falls on you it's kind of mean-spirited. It's not so nice.

"I sat down and, without drafting anything, we built a half-inch scale model right from scratch. Very low tech. Wagons. Puff of smoke. It disappears. And a stage full of people, a wonderful costume problem. I always do models. I like models. I think they're better for directors, of course. No director I ever met can read a [technical] drawing. I've been influenced by [the stage designer] Lee Simonson. I came across his work while I was at Carnegie Tech [now Carnegie Mellon]. He does isometrics and beautiful drawings. I don't have a paintbrush in my studio. I don't have a box of paint. For *Wicked* I might paint the model. But they aren't neat. I don't like neat.

"There are two classroom scenes in *Wicked*. You know classrooms are hard on stage. In the movies you can do the reverse shot. Classrooms are hard on television also. On *Saturday Night* we have to do it with the blackboard on one side and the audience sitting in profile. That's the only way in a live show you can do a cross-shot. Working in television is very different from working onstage. We should be teaching everything [about design] in school now. I think it's kind of fun. I've done rock concerts in Central Park and Africa. In Europe. Whether it's a display window, it's all connected. In good ways.

"Now, in a few weeks I have to go to Geneva, to see Harold Prince, to talk about this Sondheim musical about Addison Meisner, who was the architect and designer who basically invented the Florida gold coast. He did all that kind of Spanish architecture. And then he built factories to build the moldings. Before that he had gone to the Gold Rush. The musical is more about America. You can make money. You can lose money. You can make it again. And again and again. Reinvent yourself. I like this [musical]. And Harold had a vision. [Then] I read the novel. When I read the Sondheim lyrics and I read the script, you know I said, 'Yes, I can relate to this.' You know, it's that Henry Ford thing: if you work hard enough; it's all about work. I've been looking so hard. There are hints in the script. Like *Ragtime*. I was doing research on *Ragtime* and I came across this book on Penn Station [Pennsylvania train station in New York] and it said 'Penn Station is the portal.' And I thought, Oh, Penn Station is the portal . . . it's the proscenium. It sounds kind of literal, but why not. Then it became easy. It kind of organized the space.

"In the case of *Bounce* Prince said, 'I have this little Sondheim musical and you'd be perfect.' Then Prince said, 'You know I want to talk. Nobody wants to talk anymore. I just want to talk, talk, talk. Let's just talk a lot. [Some designers] just don't want to talk. They want to know: What do you want?' He said, 'If I knew what I wanted, I'd be a designer. I don't know what I want exactly; I just want to talk about it. I want to find a lot of research. Somewhere an [idea] will come.' And I like that. Talking is good. The things that I like the best are actor driven. What can you give them to help them do the scene?

"Years ago I could never have done a show like *Sweeney Todd* or *Ragtime* or now even *Wicked*. I didn't have a love for the so-called proscenium theatre. All of my early work, especially here in Providence with Adrian [Providence, Rhode Island, Trinity Repertory Theatre, Adrian Hall, director] has been to just destroy the proscenium, to break that down. Because you know the proscenium for the most part is just about pictures. And that seems the least interesting. Early on I did a [production of] *Slave Ship* and I walked into the theatre and said, 'Well, the first thing is: the seats have to go!' They didn't want to do that but [I thought the script] wasn't pictorial. When I did *Candide* I was always happy when the little drop with the sinking boat was in the middle of the audience. It was wonderful. When we did *Sweeney Todd* we went endlessly through New York trying to find anything that wasn't a proscenium theatre. We went to Lincoln Center. We looked at docks. We looked at warehouses.

"Scene design seems to have gotten stuck in interior design, interior decoration. I believe that set design is not interior design. It is [as much about] sculpture, or painting, or architecture for that matter. Look at the art directors in California. They were all architects before they were designers. Being a designer is one of the charms of the whole business. You know a little bit about everything, and nothing about everything.

"I began [my career] by working with Adrian Hall at Trinity Rep. And I'm still here. Must be something wrong with me. There must be something flawed in my character that makes me stay around a long time. I tend to do workshops really well. Adrian was more—maybe antiscenery—and inspired my thesis that scenery is highly overrated, because as a director he didn't care very much about what it looked like at the end of the day. He cared more about what he needed to stage the scene. What's the activity? What's needed for the actors to stage the scene? He didn't relate to the painterly [tradition]. He wanted something else. So he and I started ripping things apart.

"I always wanted to stay working at Trinity Rep. I like to work with the same people. I like this notion of the regional theatre. I spent a few months watching the Berliner Ensemble and it was very exciting. Adrian was very into [the idea of] a company of actors. You know the regional theatres built theatres that were not like New York theatres. They had a whole different goal, which I must say I approve of. New York doesn't need to be the center of theatre in this country.

"I love to go to rehearsals. I won't say I'm a frustrated director but I think that is the most exciting time. This is collaboration. Most people don't collaborate. I think the prop people should come to the rehearsal and have ideas. That does not happen anymore and that's too bad. I get production schedules and deadlines. Who wants to do a set [that way]? Wait and let me see a rehearsal. Let me talk to the actors. Maybe the actors have an idea about how it should be. I like that. This is a whole different way of working. With Andre Gregory and [the film] *Vanya on 42nd Street*, we were in rehearsal for four years. [After that] you just don't give an actor a costume. They have to like it. There has to be a lot of discussion. You just don't give Andre a set, there has to be [extended] discussion of what it might be. That's much more interesting.

"It was the same for *Saturday Night Live.* The producer couldn't find a television designer he liked so he hired me. I didn't know anything about television. I had never been in a studio before. I was doing stage design. When I went there [to do the design] I was told, 'No, no, television is done this way. You have three areas.' And I said, 'No, we're going to have stages everywhere and the cameras are going to move around.' As I've gotten older, I've gotten more flexible. Then I was not at all flexible about my ideas."

Giving the Teapot a Life

Erin Galbraith
Exhibit Designer
Washington, D.C.

The Smithsonian is the world's largest museum complex. There are over fifteen museums. Additionally there are research libraries, research institutes, and outreach programs such as the national touring exhibits described here. Erin Galbraith began her career by studying theatre design.

"My last job was a project called 'Within These Walls' for the National Museum of American History and I worked on it in two different phases. The beginning conceptual phase and then the fine-tuning and final design issues. Another designer working at the Smithsonian called me in on this project. Some of the space planning had been done. When I came onboard there was a really dense script written by four or five of the museum's curators. A theatrical script is written for the effect on an audience; this script is more about the information [to be displayed], like a book that would be published. These are academics who have spent their entire careers studying particular aspects of American history. And they write these scripts that are super dense, page after page of different descriptions and instances in history, written in a very linear fashion with text and illustrations. I have to ask, What is the story that they are trying to tell? What excites me about it? It becomes my task as a designer to unravel that a little bit and try to make it a lot more accessible.

"This was an old house that was collected from Ipswich, Massachusetts. It was disassembled and reassembled at the American History Museum. It had been on exhibit for about twenty years, [as an example of] the history of timber frame construction. It had been closed and then reopened, retelling the story of the house from the point of view of five of the families that lived in the house. The Smithsonian was interested because the house had been occupied for over 200 years by a range of families. It's a reconstructed timber frame structure about two and one-half stories tall, two stories plus an attic. It really fills the space in the museum. You walk around it; you look through the timber frame, through the walls, so there's a sense of looking through history, through transparent walls.

"In this exhibit there were so many different things going on, so many different threads to the story. We had to not only deal with the families but also with the post and beam house. The room for the first family had walls half finished so you could see the differences. So the viewer saw the horsehair, lathe, and plaster. You were seeing a room peeled back, the layers of the construction. There was also the variety of not just construction but also the furnishings of each period. But people still needed to know where to [look for the information]. This information always appeared in the same space, in the same way. We tried to be as predictable as we could. So here we tried to tone down the variety of presentation. We wanted it clean and as unobtrusive as possible.

"The five families chosen to represent the house's history included the original, rich family that had built it. The second occupants included a Brit [ish citizen] fighting on the American side for the Revolutionary War. He owned a slave and that gave us a chance to talk about slavery. Members of the third family were abolitionists and they held abolition meetings in the parlor of the house. After that, it was subdivided into apartments, and a laundress occupied one of the apartments, someone who lived and worked inside the house taking laundry into her home. The final family represented was around World War II. The mother participated in the war effort by having a 'victory garden' and collecting tin foil. She had a son who was a soldier in the war and a daughter who worked in one of the factories. The whole exhibit was about how this one house [contained] so much history and how different people used the house in different ways. The exhibit was also implying that [the viewer's] house, apartment, or street also held as much history. Originally the exhibit was going to be called 'Washington Didn't Sleep Here,' trying to gear it to the common man, the common history.

"Each exhibit begins with a script and the first part of reading the script is educating myself. I have to tease out what would be appealing to people. After reading the script I talk with the exhibit team. That process can last a good five or six months, just trying to [work through] revision after revision of the script. Just trying to get it edited down to something that was user-friendly. Part of this is learning how to let the curators know where you're going with this. A lot of the time they are not very visual people. Your job is to help them think of the exhibit in real terms. You may have to ask, 'And you expect all of this to fit on one panel?' The role that interests me the most and the role I see myself playing with the museum is: I am the translator, the conduit, for the viewer. At one point we have to talk about how the information is going to be delivered. Whether it is text rails [the small text labels that go on the cases explaining what is inside] or wall labels or panels. There are all sorts of ways of getting words across. But there are only so many words that some-one will read, without then saying, 'I'm not reading that.' They can become overwhelmed.

"Exhibit design is always about a script, the starting place. And editing, editing, editing. The groups come together with floor plans, models, text rails, and examples. We also use CAD programs that allow for fly-throughs or virtual walk-throughs that will help ex-plain our ideas to the client. There are a lot of meetings and there are a lot of debates and discussions. The sponsor of the exhibit can play a large role in this decision making. They may be [hands off] and let you do whatever you want or they may have certain expecta-tions, like the right of review.

"You have to concentrate on telling the story and telling it as succinctly as possible, coming up with other ways of helping the viewer to negotiate the exhibit. In this exhibit we had to [signal] in a really obvious way to the viewer: Okay, now you're leaving this family in the exhibit and going to the next part of the exhibit that is about a whole different family. You do this with a use of color, an obvious use of color, and icons on each panel. We use carpeting that changes so there is a sense of crossing a threshold, the beginning of each new phase of [occupancy] so again there was a clue, 'We're changing gears here.'

"By fleshing out those details we can begin to let the curators know where we're heading with the actual exhibitry [the structure of the exhibit: the cases, the text rails, the wall labels, anything that is brought into the room] and the actual audience, the viewers. There's always a back-and-forth about whether we need more infor-mation or less information. The designers always [seem to believe] less is better.

"Color always becomes very important in the design. If we use banners, we might coordinate those with the text information. We tried to be extremely consistent in keying the colors for the viewer to the [particular] family in 'Within These Walls.' I've also used color in a much more subtle way in other exhibits. I did a design for the National Yiddish Book Center (Amherst, MA) that [used] very gradual color shifts as you went from room to room. When the information was about the shtetels [Jewish villages], we used a very grayed down green, and then as we moved into the story about the war, we went into grays, and the last unit was an ashy blue. The colors can show up in a lot of areas. It can be the wall colors or banner colors or even the ink colors. In that way it is more of a subconscious thing. Very subtle.

"At the Smithsonian there is a person whose responsibility is to deal with contrasts in the exhibits so the museum will meet the guidelines for the Americans with Disabilities Act. One of her big things is contrast that is high enough to be readable, not pure white or pure black because the glare could be even worse and distracting. At the Yiddish Book Center we toned down all the contrasts. I'm thinking about the illustrations on the banners that become more tone on tone. We were trying to get a sense of reminiscence, of the feel of books, the dusty old words of the homeland.

"When we worked on the Woody Guthrie exhibit [folk singer and political activist, 1912–1967] for a Smithsonian traveling exhibit, we had to design it to pack up and move around the country. It was all about the life of Woody Guthrie. He would be writing lyrics on little pieces of paper, or doing cartoons on any piece of paper he could find. We sort of used that frenzy, that frantic note taking, as the whole line for the exhibit. Instead of square cases we used trapezoidal cases that helped make things very nonlinear. They seemed to bounce around [visually]. It was also reminiscent of the shantytowns he grew up writing about, different planes not being connected and jagged.

"We go, quite a bit, into the traffic patterns, the movement of the viewer. In 'Within These Walls' the traffic pattern was very clear, almost a forced march, because we had to think about the crowds that go through the American History Museum. On the Woody Guthrie tour exhibit, cases were set up in different patterns in different cities; we had to be careful of having each pod, each case exhibit, on its own. It had to function in whatever order you encountered it. Some people are very linear in their thinking [about exhibit design]. They want the viewer to know exactly where to go next. This is a big issue. Others are much more free-form.

"The first design exhibit I worked on was a traveling exhibit celebrating the Smithsonian Museum's 100th anniversary. Thousands of people attended. It meant forcing people through. There was a policy that anything that stopped traffic too long, any part of the exhibit, was then removed. It became demoralizing as a designer. You could be too successful. Lincoln's top hat became so popular they had to move it over to [the edges of the exhibit] to keep things moving.

"I did an exhibit for the Litchfield Law School [The Litchfield History Museum, Litchfield, CT. The Museum maintains the Tapping Reeve House and Law School, America's first law school, 1774]. Here, every line had to be extremely refined, very beautiful. It was all about penmanship. The law books were copied by hand. And the town has this remarkable [architectural] ironwork. Hand-scrolled work that they've done there forever. So we also picked up on that.

"The Litchfield project was very much about natural light. And we had to really animate the story. You know the story of America's first law school can be such a snoozer. So we used a lot of low-level lighting, a very theatrical movie to introduce the story and scrims. One of the best exhibits I ever saw was at the Norfolk, Virginia, Nautical Museum. It was a totally dark room and it was models of ships displayed on gold velvet bases and lit with one single spot from above. The models seemed to glow like little jewels. You know an exhibit about model ships could also be really dull, so they were able to give it the magic that really made it captivating.

"Exhibit design work can also be different from theatre. It's not like a director who has a vision and everyone falls in line with that vision. Collaboration varies from project to project. At the Smithsonian it was presumed the curators were running the show. Everything had to be negotiated. At the Yiddish Book Center, where they are not a museum, the designer has a lot more control. After the designers understand what [the client] wants they can say, 'We'll take it from here.' Collaboration often becomes about just person-alities, really.

"The time frame is also slower. In the theatre it's relatively quick. You have this burst of energy and then opening and then closing. At its worse, in our business, you can have an exhibit in the making for ten years. There are even examples of where the show has opened and the exhibitry is already dated. I think we spent maybe three years on 'Within These Walls.' It's not a quick burst of energy. It's a very deliberate, very reflective process.

"The actual construction is often a collaboration between the in-house fabricators and outside fabrication houses hired in. It's also permanent building structures. When we did the Smithsonian tour, the treasures, and 100th anniversary tour, the security and conservation of the objects more than any script informed the exhibit—there wasn't a story that we were telling. There were strenuous requirements. Conservation was about taking care of the object; being careful, for example, that Lincoln's hat didn't touch the case. Minnie Pearl's hat even had a special sleeve for the price tag. The crating was extraordinary. Exquisite. It was like Japanese puzzle boxes the way things came together or unfolded. The tour required something like twenty-two trucks.

"Because there were so many parts of the Smithsonian, galleries and collections, the idea was not to separate out the treasures and identify them from each collection but to establish some universal themes: remembering, discovering, and imagining. Remembering was the historical, discovering was more the scientific artifacts, and imagining was the art and the design, like jewelry and sculpture. So we designed three galleries. Each gallery had its own look, its own color scheme, and a different focus. But each gallery had a similar entrance area [design] to tie it together.

"With collaboration, you have to go into the process with a real healthy respect for the curators. They've spent their whole lives [with the material], the [archival] work. You need to help them visualize where you're going with the design. I realized if I brought in a sketch or talked to them in a way they could see where I was going, that helped a lot. You know a lot of people look at a floor plan and have no idea what they're looking at. They don't think like that. And I'm sure we drove them crazy. 'You got your facts wrong.' There's a lot of back-and-forth. If you want them onboard you have to walk them through very slowly and very carefully. It can't be interior design. They can't worry that we're dumbing down the information or that it's just a fluff piece. Being that conduit actually interests me more than designing the actual case or other parts of the exhibitry. I want to give the teapot a life."

About Three Buttons

Robert Blackman
Costume Designer
Television, film, and stage

Star Trek *remains one of the longest running franchises on television, starting with the original series in 1966. Blackman joined* Star Trek: The Next Generation *as costume designer for its third season and went on to design every episode of* Star Trek: Deep Space Nine *and* Star Trek: Voyager. *He also designed the feature film* Star Trek: Generations. *He currently designs* Enterprise. *He is the recipient of an Emmy award for his designs and has been nominated nine times. Blackman is a graduate of the Yale School of Drama.*

"This is the fourth series that I've done with the *Star Trek* group, but my process, I think, remains the same no matter what medium I'm working in. What does change is the perception of scale and that's where the difference is for me. The closer you get, the smaller it can be. It would be the same issue on stage [whether] you were doing a 300-seat arena production or a 1,300-seat amphitheatre. Character detail becomes smaller. My part of it changes only in how I have to approach the viewing surface. It's really about the viewing surface. If you're going to see a head forty feet across, as in film, with only a tie and a shirt collar, well that's going to look different than if you're seeing that actor's head from forty feet away [in the theatre] or if you're seeing it on a fourteen-inch screen.

"There is also the scale of time. With television it gets smaller; there's less time for the story. There's more time in film and theatre. Also film tends to shoot [out of sequence]. The end is [shot at] the beginning; the beginning is [shot at] the end. And if you are dealing with nonvisual people, there is the problem of explaining your design arc to them. The sense of progression in the design is out of order in the shooting. You have to spend a few days making them understand how the design goes [to the final point]. [The actors] shouldn't look at the end like they looked at the beginning. It's not that [the producers] are bad or can't figure it out, it's just another way of thinking. It becomes your job as the designer to figure this out for these various media.

"There are certain rules you learn or tricks you find to help you through this but what I find is I have to remember the actor. You know, right now you can be less detailed in television work but the movement to digital will change that. We shoot *Star Trek* in 16-mm film and then transfer to tape so there is some loss [of detail]. Digital TV will help prevent the degradation, called 'stepped down,' that we have to deal with now. I found that I couldn't reduce the level of detail, however, because of the actor. It's still real to them. Do they really want to look at a hem that has staples in it? No. They want to see that the garment is as real as possible.

"This really comes from my training. It's about the actor and it's about interpretation. The design part of it is very important. But none of that can happen until I have a clear understanding of what the script is about, until I can understand what kind of story the writers and producers are trying to tell. Television is easier. It's very straightforward. With the series there's very little prep time. Time gets compressed and concentrated. Nobody gets the kind of time you can get when you're doing a feature or a film. I have to be able to read the script in one pass or two passes and get all there is because that's all the time I have. [The methods for studying the script] are just in my head. What are the indicators that will help tell the story in pictures rather than words? It may be the tone of a scene. I may call up and say [to the writers or the producers], 'This reads this way, am I misinterpreting or is that the way you want to go with it?'

"You know years ago, producers didn't get it; they didn't understand that designers could actually read scripts and interpret them. They just thought 'Read the script and find a nice skirt because that's what we want.' So I had no problem telling them I thought there was more the costume could do, more that could be said. Then they got it and realized there was no threat involved, that I wasn't going to be critical of the script. As a designer I have to work in the generalized form and way writers work. We look for the thesis; we figure out how to tell the story. [As designers] we aren't doing it with words or with camera angles, we're doing it with buttons and bows or whatever. It's about interpreting the script, figuring out what that is, and coming up with your best shot at how to tell that story. Sometimes there can be lots of nuance in that. Do the producers want to do it boldly? Or very subtly? It's about getting to know who you're dealing with.

"One of the real values, for me artistically, of these long-term projects, like the series, is getting to know the people. There is always the question, 'Do I want to spend the next seven years with these people?' It's like taking a cross-country car trip in a station wagon with all these people. We do twenty-six episodes and at about episode eighteen I begin to feel we are somewhere in [the middle of the country]. The trip has become boring; it's getting ugly. It's not good. But if you can get through it, it becomes like a family. The family has its different moods and modes, depending on the day. There's a ton of pressure on the producers and the writers. I think they know I understand that; I get it and I want what would be best for the show and what would be best for that episode and how do we make sure that the overall ideas that we've talked about get across.

"Now that can be very vague. In episodics, the overall arc can change, or you may not be picked up for the next season and of course there are always the demographics. We respond to the viewers. Episodic television is being in the trenches. It just is. Everyone is there and in the trenches. You know that if the ratings drop, there's going to be some big change.

"We have to deal also with stunt casting. That's where we will have a 'name' in a role that week. The most successful introductions are with classically trained actors who come on and play these very peculiar aliens. These actors seem to be able to strike a note between unique and human, human being the common denominator. Part of it is the chameleon-like nature of the training. They're able to do Shakespeare. They aren't afraid of mustaches and wigs and hats, so they're not afraid of [alien] costumes. These actors don't count on the uniqueness of 'you as you' [as with stars].

"You know in television it's about the neck up. No matter how great the set is, no matter how great the clothes are, or the other aspects are, and so on, what you ultimately focus on is the actor's face. And this is true in theatre, film, and television. You have to be able to see their faces. You have to be able to see their lips so you can understand what they are saying, to hear the obscure Shakespearean references. You have to be able to see their eyes so you can see all that inner working of the character. Onstage you want to draw focus to the face and the hands. In the old days you would put white gloves on the character. The face and the hands are the actors' [tools] for telling the story. The same thing happens in television but the scale, again, gets pulled down. You have to be careful in television that you don't spend your time on this amazing, hand-embroidered thing around the actor's neck because then the audience spends their time looking at that; they're not looking at the actor's eyes.

"Or it can go the other way. There is such an influence of music videos in the directing now. They tend to go in so tight and shoot from the Adam's apple to the forehead. There's [a certain fear] to go with a waist shot or a cowboy shot where the gun holster could be seen. Or a full shot where you see the whole figure. These [tight shots] tend to get overused. It's too much. If the camera lens is three inches away, max, then maybe the actor will become self-conscious. 'Now I act?' It may not work.

"So many producers now have no theatre experience. They don't know the actor's process. They don't know how actors work. But they do know where they want focus, and a tight shot [is a way] of getting that focus.

"We define character rank by color. On *Star Trek*, because there are so many special effects—and on this new series the uniforms are blue—we only can use green screen. We could use orange screen but special effects people don't like it. They can't get as much detail as with the green screen. They will color correct away from green toward blue."

Blackman is referring to the photographic, now digital, process known as chroma-key. Actors are photographed against a solid color background (blue, green, or orange) that is then optically removed and another background substituted.

"So color for me is no longer as viable because I never know what it's going to end up being. I can't define character so much with color any more. So silhouette and texture become more important for me. I use those in every single moment of my thought process as a designer.

"Because we have, in this series, the ongoing saga of these particular people, because they are what they are and they are going to be in these uniforms, then the people that come to visit [the starship] are either in things that are contrary to the uniforms so the heroes always stand out or something so they don't ever blend in. So it becomes vinyl suits or heavily textured suits, leather suits that are beaten and quilted and all that stuff I've done for years. There has to be, at a glance, what I call photo recognition. At a glance, you know that these people are different [from the crew]. There has to be that separation between them. Every once in a while we'll have someone who comes from an earth-based society so we can do character in the old way, much subtler. Let's say we're in a bank. There is a character that wants to get ahead, so they dress a certain way. It's all within a very tight format. So instead of it being about leather, it becomes about pocket protectors and ties. It becomes about very small details that tell this person from that person. With alien races we don't know those subtleties. We don't know what they are. If we have the chance to keep a group of aliens around long enough we can start deconstructing them, giving them more nuances of character, the rebels within the group, and so on.

"The silhouettes for the aliens become indications of physical form as well as character traits. We usually begin with just suit construction and things like shoes; as we get to know them we may see more of the actual [body].

"[In the costume designs] there are the basics. Usually warm colors are a higher temperature, just like emotions. You will see that. Cooler colors, the opposite. How open or closed up are the characters' [costumes]? Is that about some kind of protection? Or quirkiness? If the neck is open they may seem more vulnerable. If we can see the trachea area, that connects to the heart. But, of course, you can go too far with that. If the openness goes below the sternum, it may suddenly become more provocative. It's really about three buttons, how you button or unbutton the shirt. It can be buttoned up to the neck. Or unbuttoned just to the trachea. Or to the sternum. We start making certain value judgments about the character based on that [degree of exposure]. I always want the uniforms to be more open, to open them up to make the characters seem more human, more vulnerable. So that we as the audience can relate in a more personal way to them."

Index

Mach 1/3/08